CENTER STAGE

Jim Neglia

authorHOUSE®

AuthorHouse™
1663 Liberty Drive
Bloomington, IN 47403
www.authorhouse.com
Phone: 1 (800) 839-8640

Published by AuthorHouse 01/10/2019

ISBN: 978-1-5462-7507-7 (sc)
ISBN: 978-1-5462-7508-4 (hc)
ISBN: 978-1-5462-7506-0 (e)

Library of Congress Control Number: 2019900243

Print information available on the last page.

This book is printed on acid-free paper.

"The world is a looking glass and gives back to every man the reflection of his own face." ~William Makepeace Thackeray

January 29, 2013 11:47:22 p.m.

When I see my friends posting pictures on social media while they are away on trips abroad, my inner senses awaken. As I look scroll through my feed and look at the pictures, no matter where they were taken, I imagine myself standing in their shoes. No matter if it was taken in the middle of a square, a market, on a bridge, or near a waterway, I feel instantly transported.

As the feelings of travel saturate my mind, I can quickly relive and feel my past experiences as if they were happening all over again. Entirely within my memories, lost in thought just the same, as if a symphonic movement is coming to a grand climax. I find myself both breathless and frozen, simultaneously.

I cannot articulate the feeling because I cannot fully understand the transformation itself. What I do know is that the same sense of oneness with every village, city, and town is rooted deep within me and this same emotion returns to me time and time again.

Later the same night: 1:27:15 a.m.

I always knew when I was growing up that someday, I would write a book. I always had the urge to write, but didn't know what the final push would be in making my dream into a reality.

My wife suggested I go through my diary, my work files, and pull out some of the juiciest stories to share. She suggested that I start there and see where it took me by the end of the month.

Those were the words I needed to hear to motivate me. I no longer thought that writing a book was an insurmountable task. Instead, it was a goal I felt that was now within my grasp.

Considering the topics I would share, I knew I want to highlight some of the most important people in my life, as well as those crossroads moments I took along the way. Stories of mishaps, emotionally challenging moments, as well as a message of following your dream, are central to my story.

Publishing the book is perhaps one of the most significant accomplishments of my life, to date. Not only did I cross a major item off my "to do," bucket list, but I was also able to demonstrate to our sons the importance of dedication. Both Phillip (our 19-year-old and Daniel (our 8-year-old) witnessed first-hand the commitment of a project of such magnitude come to fruition. On December 19, 2012, less than one year from the beginning, my first book was published. Daniel thinks I am a literary genius, to this day.

During the writing process, my emotions were running on high, morning, noon and night. I wrote the majority of the book between the hours of midnight and 4:00 a.m., after our sons were asleep and I had tucked my wife under the down comforter hours earlier. All of that came to a crashing halt sometime about 11 months into the writing process, and soon, a new, unrecognizable depression hit me.

I was left with a tremendous amount of creative energy and nowhere to use it. What's next for me, what can I do? What are other projects out there waiting for me? I began to think and think; the symphony wasn't enough! I questioned my ability: "*Could* I write another book?"

Music plays a large part in my creative process, as it enhances my desire to express myself through written words. During these creative spurts, I recognized the highlights of my life, which consists of writing and musical stimulation.

Music helps propel me back in my memory bank. Music mixed with raw emotion allows me to share the details of past experiences in real time.

When writing, I am literally "in" the moment. My brain tells my fingers which keys to press and off they go, transcribing the feelings in my head.

Often, while still in a deeply reflective state after a long writing session, I gaze into my innermost personal self. Tonight, I am thinking about my materialistic side and the word "possessions." I know, that aspect of my life is nearly nonexistent. The need for more has dissipated, especially over the past few years. This has been a fantastic realization and change that has affected me and my thinking process, immensely over the past few years.

I know with absolute certainty, I am in no need of a bigger house, a more expensive car, or flashy jewelry. I don't need to have more things. Things require a place to put them, more shelves, more desk surface, and more living space. I prefer to keep my needs and living style to a minimum.

My needs have decreased dramatically to the basics: a place for my family to live, food on the table, clothes on our backs, and a means of reliable transportation.

Some spend a lot of time and energy looking after their belongings. By having fewer things to look after, life naturally becomes more manageable and indeed less cluttered. By having less totality, I have less to consider, less to think about, and less to concern me. This frees my mental capacity to make room other things: my relationships, my family, friends, colleagues, and even the guy up the block.

Having a job like mine, it aids to have less to consider in my home life as well. When I come home from work, our house is set up in a very orderly, fashion. In our case, less *is* more. I am fortunate to have a partner who shares the same thoughts and vision as I do."

Reviewing this journal entry, I penned a few years ago, I realized those feelings encompass every aspect of my life, less is more. I have a longing to learn what can only be acquired through the experiences, and not from stories written in books.

Coming to America

"Your life does not get better by chance. It gets better by change."
~Jim Rohn

While working for a local Arts organization, I was asked if I knew anyone in the field who immigrated to this country. I didn't need to search my mind long before coming up with the right person. Alexandra Gorokhovsky was not only the perfect subject for the organization's exposé, but she also happened to be the woman who I would soon marry.

With pleasure and great promise, I asked Alexandra if she would be interested in sharing her story. Without hesitation, she agreed and on that fateful day in mid-October, we sat down at Tops Diner, shared a meal and began our interview.

Your Name and instrument Alexandra Gorokhovsky, violin

What country are you from? Russia

When did you come to America? On October 12, 1989, my parents, younger sister and I departed from Russia and through immigration process traveled via Vienna and Rome. The first time I set foot in America was on February 2, 1990, nearly four months after our departure.

What made you decide to leave your country? There are three primary reasons for our family's departure. The first may be the most essential or most thought-provoking: the catastrophe at Chernobyl made an enormous impact on my father's thinking. After Chernobyl, my father, at the age of 41, had a heart attack and spent time in the hospital under horrible care. He decided that if he ever came close to recovery, he would leave Kiev, regardless of his future health. The third reason was that we are Jewish and we were living in an area where anti-Semitism was extremely high. It was my father who didn't see any future for us, as a persecuted Jewish family to continue.

Since the first grade, I lived with the discomforts of my Jewish faith. Constantly reminded I was a Jew and living in a Communist country, I knew I would never be allowed to enter a proper conservatory or live my life with the same chances as others. It was time to find a new beginning and promise of a new life.

What have been the benefits? The answer to this question is straightforward: freedom of expression, freedom to choose a proper college, school, and place of work. The level of life in the United States is so much higher than the suppression I lived under while in Russia.

In Russia, the government itself had just collapsed, and we didn't know what to expect. When we arrived in the United States, we weren't sure what to expect but knew there was so much more we would be offered then what we had left in the old country.

What was your "dream of America" and has it come true? Our dream was to work and live peacefully knowing our family was safe and able to express ourselves in freedom. To express myself in a way I wanted to, rather, needed. To be able to work with an orchestra and perform at the highest level attainable was always at the forefront of my mind. I never knew if I would have the opportunity to shine in the United States, but soon learned that my goals were attainable. Additionally, to know deep down inside that, I will always have options with all aspects of my life was incredibly comforting.

Most fascinating is the thought to be able to shop in a store with full shelves. I couldn't imagine what it was like not to have to stand in a line for 6 hours for a pint of milk or a loaf of bread. By coming to America, our dreams will come true.

How is America different than what you thought it would be?

It is not that it is different from what I imagined; I didn't know what to expect. In Russia, my family never left our city, I never traveled abroad and had no idea what was in store for me. We just knew in our hearts; we were leaving Russia for a better life. By moving, we had nothing to lose except our possession. Incidentally, we were not permitted to take any belongings with us regardless of how we persisted. A small price to pay for the beautiful life we learned in America.

What is your favorite American food? Holiday? Seafood is my favorite, soft shell crabs in particular – what a fantastic discovery. My favorite holiday without hesitation is New Year's Eve, a time where we can reflect on the past and then wish each other all the blessings of what is to come.

Anything else you care to share with me about your experience? I have had challenging moments in my life and had only my parents to rely on while growing up. As long as they had their health, I knew we would be fine. After my father's heart attack, we knew, for the safety of our family, it was time to leave Russia and pursue a new and better life.

My parents taught me always to be an optimistic, happy, and cheerful person while keeping in mind to be dedicated to life itself and those in my family. This attitude has been translated into my love of all and the needs to help those around me. At this moment in time, I am entirely comfortable living a very happy life with my family here in Brooklyn.

Happy 50th

"Music gives a soul to the universe, wings to the mind,
flight to the imagination and life to everything" -Plato

Journal entry: August 25, 2013

Although I have traveled a great deal in my life, I still have grand aspirations to travel more. I adore the art of travel in its most profound meaning. I love the ability to discover that comes about from any trip: exploring new countries, cities, museums, mountain chains, cultures and, of course, the people.

As I was planning my 50th birthday celebration trip, I had an epiphany of sorts. Well, not a spiritual manifestation of Christ to the Gentiles as represented by the Magi, but an absolute realization which moved me deeply. It happened while I was mapping out our travel route of nearly 2000 miles. I felt for the first time in almost 50 years my desires to visit, if not live in, Europe.

I come from firmly European roots, as my family comes from the small city of Enna, Sicily. I, along with my siblings, are the first-generation Italian Americans to live here in the United States.

I made the journey back to visit Enna some years ago, and while reflecting on that visit, memories came flooding back. Visions of my footsteps through Enna's Town Hall, where my great uncle Francesco Paolo's theater is located. The overwhelming feeling, I have always possessed about my love of music, art, the culture was now coming to the forefront of my mind. I had experienced this feeling many times over the course of my life, but only once before on a level as deep as this.

My first visit to Vienna was so moving it brought me to a level of intense exhilaration. As we pulled into the city and the doors of the train opened, I set foot on the Ringstraße (Ringstrasse). As my foot hit the cobblestones below, I nearly lost my balance. My knees went weak as I felt, with absolute certainty, the history beneath my shaking feet.

As I lifted my eyes, I saw across the street was the famous Wiener Staatsoper, The Vienna State Opera House. The building was completed in the mid-19th century, which means that so many extraordinarily talented and recognizable musicians graced the stage, orchestra pit. All I could think about was Gustav Mahler standing outside the theater, smoking a pouch of tobacco before entering to conduct.

Herbert von Karajan was thought to be the top-selling classical music recording artist of all time, having sold an estimated 200 million records. Other brilliant minds such as Felix Weingartner, Richard Strauss, Bruno Walter, Maria Callas, Luciano Pavarotti, Leonard Bernstein, Fritz Reiner, Hans Richter, Claudio Abbado, and so many others came to mind immediately. Just the thought that such incredible musicians graced this hall with their unbelievable and unique talent was overwhelming. It was by far one of the most memorable days of my life.

Having the primary hotel locations in place, I began plotting side trip to nearby destinations. From Stresa, we would visit Nozzolino, Ascona, Verbania, Mont Brè, Locarno, Orselina, Lugano, and Cannobio. On our drive to Croatia, we would pass through Slovenia and cross back into Italy, where we could stop in Trieste. Just a short drive from Innsbruck is the hauntingly beautiful Berchtesgaden in Germany. These were only a few of the side trips we planned for our celebratory visit to Europe.

Long before we departed, I decided I would focus on keeping a thorough account of all events, experiences, and sights along the way. Documenting every aspect of the experience was essential to me. I enjoy the art of writing so much that I gave serious consideration to which pencil I use, as well as how sharp a point was needed to write.

My initial thought was to wake every morning before my family and go down to the veranda to grab a cup of coffee and begin documenting what took place the day before. Doing so, would allow me one night to sleep on my thoughts and reflect on what took place the day before.

Reflecting on the reasonable success of *Onward and Upward*, I thought to myself, should I attempt a sequel? If so, I would use the vacation notes as part of the story, no? Considering carefully, I questioned, can I see myself dedicating another year of my life and energy on such an enormous task? I had mixed feelings.

As the foundation for the book, I settled on the idea of cranking out a thorough account of our August 2013 trip. I knew then that I needed to devote my time and energy towards this particular goal. I needed to document the events of my fiftieth celebration tour.

Although my mind was made up, and a second book was forthcoming, I was living a very involved work life. I was going to do my best to balance out my fast-paced work life and family obligations with my promise of a second book.

While transcribing the notes of the travel portion of this book, some 24,000 handwritten words, and thoughts remain in focus. I tried not to think about what was happening in my daily work life. Motivated to split my attention on the "current state of work affairs" as well as our trip, I made sure to be thorough in both areas.

Travel journal, pencil, sharpener, and eraser, summer of 2013

Reflecting on my task, I understand that writing about our current trip was an exercise in discipline. I am going to share that while spending time in Europe, I found myself split nearly down the middle while writing each journal entry. I make a concerted effort to divide my travel journal in half, thus allowing me to add notes to my current, past and possible future work in my industry all while compiling notes from my daily travels. However, writing about the rest caused me much anxiety, pain, reflection, and tedious documentation of thoughts I did not want to confront. Facing and working through a dark period is the exact opposite of the enjoyment I was living while traveling throughout Europe. Thus, the juxtaposition persisted.

I knew a new period was knocking at my door; I just needed to respond to the quest. Questions of divine intervention that will be answered in the years ahead of me. There were new adventures ever so close; if I only knew. I didn't want to put a damper on my holidays but found myself documenting uncertain times in the arts, as well as my personal growing doubts of my continuation in the industry. Reflecting back, I can see how this discord has offered me so much opportunity for growth.

We designed this particular trip around two things: my family and a particular travel route. The plan was to reach multiple regions and explore them the best we could. Beginning in Switzerland and heading south to Stresa, Italy which sits on the banks of Lake Maggiore. From there, we would continue southeast to Milan, Verona, and Venice seeking sanctuary in Venice for three nights.

Continuing eastward and heading to Opatija, Croatia passing through Trieste, Italy, and Slovenia. From the Adriatic coast, we would move northward to Salzburg. A day trip from Salzburg to Český Krumlov was in order, without question. Ultimately Salzburg took us west to Innsbruck, which led to our final destination of Zurich, before departing for the airport to go back home to Newark.

I had always fantasized about a trip with such possibilities, but this time, I made the fantasy come to fruition the moment we purchased the airline tickets, through careful planning many months prior to departure.

The most critical piece of the puzzle was to determine which city we would start our European experience in. After checking with our friends at the frequent flyer offices of the Chase Sapphire card, we learned that we had enough points in our bank to cover all four round-trip tickets to Zurich from Newark International Airport. Our plans were firming up!

With tickets in hand, it was time to make the hotel reservations. Once again, using all the resources afforded me, I scoured the internet. I began to make the necessary reservations to accommodate our family of four. Within hours, grand hotels in all locations - confirmed.

Just as we were circling the counties on our itinerary, I feel that my life is coming around, nearly full circle. Change is imminent, I knew it, better yet, I felt it.

Chance Meeting

"There are chance meetings with strangers that interest us from the first moment before a word is spoken." ~Fyodor Dostoevsky

When I joined the orchestra in 1998, I first saw my future wife sitting in the seat directly in front of me, in the violin section. During that same period of time, I was already enjoying a healthy freelance performance career as well as a hectic contracting schedule.

I vividly remember needing help with a Russian-to-English score translation, when one of my freelance orchestras were preparing to perform the Carmen Suite of Bizet, arrangement by Rodion Shchedrin. Shchedrin is a distinguished musician who came from a Russian musical family.

Because of the vastness of the percussion solo parts, I was drawn to this arrangement and wanted to learn all I could about the annotations throughout the score. This arrangement calls for five solo percussionists, as well as a supporting string orchestra, a solo xylophone, marimba, vibraphone, tubular chimes, and glockenspiel, which perform all melodies of each movement. The strings are, for the first time in my musical memory, just accompaniment for the percussion soloists. Finally, a chance for us to shine!

During all symphony rehearsals, work rules affords us a 20-minute break somewhere in the middle of our two-and-a-half-hour call. It was during one of these breaks that I sat next to Sasha. I leaned over and asked if she wouldn't mind translating the Cyrillic directions in my printed score so I can better understand their meaning. Without pause, she agreed, and in consideration of the short amount of time we had, we got right to it.

Most of the directions in the percussion score had much to do with what mallet or stick we needed to perform certain passages. Listed in multiple places was С металлической щеткой – which means "with wire brush" and С мягкой коляской, meaning "with a soft mallet." I would never have known the translations as this episode took place in the year 1999. At that time, there was no such thing as Google, nor were there any translation sites on the World Wide Web.

Alexandra, who affectionately went by the nickname Sasha, was eager to help and share with me many other translations, as well. Thinking of her helpfulness, I remember thinking how kind and caring she was to spend this time with me.

She translated every phrase I requested, and before we know it, not only was our break over, but my score was complete. I never forgot her generosity, not for a moment. Little did we know, one day we would share more than score translations.

Over the years, I began working with the symphony more frequently. At the same time, my contracting work was expanding rapidly. I couldn't help but see that I was consistently finding myself in the right place at the right time.

Some years ago, in the summer of 1998, during a musical tour of Spain, I met a man named Everett. During the tour, he learned that I was a contractor in the New York/New Jersey area. Everett asked me if I would be willing to hire the musicians needed for a performance of the Fauré

Requiem. The concert was set to take place in a few months at New York's prestigious Carnegie Hall.

I agreed and upon my arrival back to the United States, I presented him with a very competitive budget.

After considering all I had to offer, Everett ultimately secured me to hire the Fauré orchestra.

At the first meeting of Field Studies (who secured Everett and his chorus) we needed to finalize the rehearsal schedule and logistics of the event. It was during this session that the production manager and I struck up mutual respect for each other.

A few months after the success of the Fauré, Field Studies asked me to secure the musicians needed for all their upcoming events, a total of eight concerts. These performances would not require a full orchestra, but just a handful of accompanying players, one of which was Sasha.

That year, there was a higher than a typical number of events to contract, and by chance, the most requested musicians during this particular year were violins. I employed Sasha, as well as a few others, to perform on all of the upcoming services.

There was a great deal of work and income for any freelance musician, never mind the contractor. Everyone was happy as we were all keeping very busy.

My last performance in 2005 of the Carnegie Hall series fell on April 3. I remember this date so vividly because it was the day that I rediscovered the beauty of Alexandra Gorokhovsky, her sincere warmth, poise, and musicianship.

On April 3, I pulled up to a vacant parking spot on 56th Street, just one block west of 7th Avenue. As I placed the car in park, I looked in my rearview mirror only to see Sasha pulling into the spot directly behind me. In 2005, New York City allowed a person to park their car for just a 2-hour period before having to add more time to the meter.

It was about 5 p.m. when we arrived, and her sound check was set to begin at 6 p.m., with the performance commencing at 8 p.m.

I stepped out of my car, and as I turned to my left, I saw her stepping out of hers at the same time. We both chuckled at the coincidence as we started our walk to the hall. We talked about the dreaded meters as we strolled, since as we knew we were going to have to feed them several times that evening to avoid getting a ticket.

Once inside the hall, we were so absorbed into our conversation, time seemed to lose meaning. In fact, we came dangerously close to missing the sound check window, due to our incessant conversation.

After she had completed her sound-checks, we still had a good deal of time to kill before the performance. We sat down together and picked up our conversation where we left off, without pause.

Since Sasha is a native of the Ukraine, English is not her strong language. On this night though, I felt it was her primary, even native tongue. She spoke with complete articulation, feeling, and comprehension.

Our conversation covered everything from work, to family, kids, parents, gigs, and life in general. I learned that she had traveled to Hartford, Connecticut about 125 miles one way, for many years and she learned that I spent eight years commuting to Harrisburg, Pennsylvania, about 180 miles away. We both endured that grueling commute for many years until we settled into our current positions.

So many parallels existed between us, yet we hailed from two polar opposite worlds, quite literally. The United States and Ukraine were nowhere geographically near each other, nor were they ideologically in the same ballpark. However, after talking, we learned just how close we both agreed with our core beliefs.

I found myself becoming more attracted to her voice, her thoughts, her accent, and indeed, her charm and beautiful disposition. I remember looking into her eyes thinking, how is it possible I can have so much in common with a "foreigner?"

Well, she was a foreigner in the eyes of geography, but as far as I was concerned, she was perhaps the most interesting person I had ever met. I was intrigued by her conversation, command of the English language, intoxicating beauty, dark skin, brown eyes; it all started to become a blur.

"Stop it, Jim, just stop it," I thought to myself on several occasions during our talk, but my infatuation grew. Not a high school infatuation, but an adult feeling, one which pushed me to new and undiscovered areas I had never experienced before.

Nearly 8 p.m., her performance time was now upon us, and we were off to the backstage area. Putting on my contractor's hat, I had her take her place just off stage, in what I call "the batter's box." The time had come, and the stagehand opened the sizeable white door leading out to Isaac Stern Auditorium. Sasha gave a top-notch performance, and I was impressed by her, professional demeanor and sense of humility.

While packing up her violin back in the green room, she tilted her head ever so slightly to the right and asked: "Would like to have a glass of wine?" I accepted.

Looking at the time, we ran out to our back to back parked cars and added 1 ½ hours to our meters; I noted the time, it was 9:33 p.m. I took my receipt and tossed it in the front of my 325i windshield. There it sat, in anticipation of what was to come.

We walked just a few paces east from the stage door and found ourselves sitting comfortably at the New Topaz Thai Restaurant, sitting in a very quiet booth just a few feet from the main entranceway.

Our conversation once again picked up where our backstage chat ended. Spending this time with her only affirms my feelings for Sasha. "No Jim, no," I told myself. "I am the personnel manager of the symphony; I cannot date a member of the orchestra, I just can't." I struggled with my thoughts but decided to push them aside for the time being.

Hours had passed in what felt like a single moment, but glancing at my watch, I saw that it was nearly 11:30. We both knew that our muni-meters were about to expire and didn't want to suffer the expense of a New York City parking meter violation.

We called the waiter to our table and asked for the bill. Once we squared the check away, we darted up the block to our waiting cars. Good news, no tickets!

I motioned for her to join me in my car for a nightcap of conversation. Keeping an eye on the rearview mirror for meter maids, we continued talking. We were both happy, content, feeling silly, and enjoying the moment.

At that moment, we both noticed that for the first time all evening, the conversation came to a sudden stop. Not sure what to do, or what to say, I just waited, as did Sasha. The tension was electrifying, a great feeling of want, need, and without question, desire.

Not sure what to say, I turned to her and said, "We must have good luck together because we don't have tickets on our cars." She smiled with an awkward acknowledgment. I sensed that my remarks might have been empty, my gosh, now what? I am 42 years old and feel like a teenager. It was at that moment that I realized with certainty that I liked this woman. I liked her more than I thought I liked her. I acknowledged that it was not just a wine induced feeling, but one of actual consequence.

I knew our time this evening had to come to an end, it was late, and we both needed to get home. A few glasses of wine after a busy few weeks at the symphony and Carnegie engagements, we were exhausted, not thinking clearly. All this crossed my mind, several times until I lifted my chin and saw that our eyes met, I said the magic words, "Get home safely, goodnight."

I moved forward to kiss her on her cheek, but as I did, her head tilted forward, and her soft lips were on mine.

D.O.T. Parking Stub from our Chance Meeting

Best Friends

"A friend is one that knows you as you are, understands where you have been, accepts what you have become, and still, gently allows you to grow." ~ William Shakespeare

As I would stay up, night after night in my dimly lit office, Sasha never said a word. Instead, my wife offered silent understanding and acceptance of the task at hand.

As I reflect on the past, she had firsthand experience of seeing just down the hallway from our bedroom my office light spilling out from behind the partially closed door. She had lived through the same scenario back in 2012, while I was writing my first book, of the many nights I would flop into bed at 4 a.m., after hours spent behind the keyboard.

She possesses patience beyond most, patience learned as a person who has been exposed to strict discipline, severe studies and dedication to one's craft, through playing the violin. Her commitment and drive have revealed itself into precisely who she is to this day.

Her father chose the violin for her because he saw it as an instrument which he always liked and wanted to share his passion with his daughter.

She and her father both had a dedication that far surpasses most student's desire, much less understanding. He felt that there was a real need to have her excel in the abilities which are required to push a musician to a performance career of the highest possible level.

As Sasha grew as a player, her father became increasingly more dedicated as her mentor in music. After years of scales, arpeggios, and smaller pieces fell under her fingers; the desire to push her further ran a strict parallel to his life. Marik, being an accomplished Bayan player himself, had the talent to instill all of his knowledge into his star pupil.

He never relented; day after day, week after week and then, year after year, he explained to her how to play, how to phrase, how to make music. With each soloistic work, his determination became even stronger. As each genre of music became part of her repertoire, ingrained in her fingertips, musicality, and love, her father would feel the absolute sense of accomplishment of his work, as well as their work together.

This would prove to be one of his most significant accomplishments, as by the time they immigrated to America, Sasha was prepared to win a position with a major symphony orchestra.

If it weren't for her father's intense dedication, Sasha and I never would have met. We joke at times that Sasha had to come from Kiev to settle in Brooklyn, only to win a position with the Orchestra. A few short years later, I would begin my work with the same orchestra, and together, we found that our love of music and life ran in complete harmony.

Circles

"For once you have tasted flight, you will walk the earth
with your eyes turned skywards, for there you have been and
there you will long to return." ~Leonardo da Vinci

August 8, Day 1 *Flight from Newark International Airport in New Jersey
to Zurich, Switzerland. Departure time, 9:55 p.m.*

August 9, Day 2 *Land Zurich, pick up the rental car and drive to Stresa,
Italy - 250 Kilometers*

We departed as scheduled, 21:55 and landed a little ahead of schedule at
12:30 local time, the following afternoon.

Usually, I can sleep without issue on trips overseas, especially on flights
which depart at such a late hour. On this particular flight, I woke up
at about 4 a.m. United States time, which was bizarre and entirely
uncharacteristic of me. I was perplexed until my half-asleep brain caught
up to my conscious mind. The only thought that penetrated my groggy
skull was the art of journal keeping. I could not avoid or dismiss the firm
commitment I had made before the trip to document the days and weeks
to come.

As I fully awoke, I realized and understood that I must unequivocally follow through on this specific goal. Having spent much of the past 30 years documenting life events, I knew the magnitude of the task set before me and took it to heart. That very thought woke me from my sleep to what I believe was to serve as a harsh reminder.

The months I spend preparing for the total travel experience itself were both critical and exhilarating. I love absorbing the visually stimulating pictures sprinkled throughout the internet, taking notice of the destinations awaiting us. The process of preparing, not only educates me, but also helps construct a varied travel experience. I base our final itinerary on all these factors, along with our collective desire to experience specific cities. In all cases, preparation is vital!

Regarding our pending 50th birthday trip, I was making adjustments up until the very last minute. I changed the hotel in Venice as well as Croatia a few times. In Venice, I swapped out one hotel for another as we ultimately decided to stay further away from the high tourist area of Saint Marco Square. As for Croatia, initially we were to stay in Rijeka, but recently I moved our stay to the resort town of Opatija. I made this decision based on a suggestion from a friend who has traveled the world five times over.

In both cases, I am curious to see how well these plans will impact our trip. We will have to wait until the days we arrive in both cities to see the outcome. I made a note of the address of the original hotel in Venice as I did in Rijeka as I knew we would visit Rijeka during our stay in Croatia.

By this time, my mind was racing with thoughts. Knowing that there was no way I could fall back asleep, I hit the button on the top left of the panel of my armrest signaling for the flight attendant. Once she appeared, I requested a cup of coffee. While the flight attendant poured the coffee, I pulled out my trusty journal and began documenting my thoughts.

Flight 7701 UA, Swiss Air landed, and now, the real adventures were about to begin.

Disembarking the plane, retrieved our luggage, went through customs, and then proceeded to the car rental area to pick up our waiting car. Although we had reserved a specific vehicle, the salesman informed us that there were other options to consider. Would we like a diesel or regular fuel car, manual or automatic transmission, full-size or midsize as well as trunk size? All of these standard questions fell on somewhat deaf ears as I was feeling the effects of the journey and lack of sleep.

When push came to shove, we kept our initial reservation, a mid-

size, manual transmission, and four-door car with only one change. We opted for the diesel gas car, as we learned that diesel was less expensive in all of the countries we were going to visit except Switzerland. Our new plan to save a few euros was to gas up at the end of the trip before crossing the Liechtenstein-Swiss border. Once in Switzerland, we would top off the tank just outside the airport, saving money along the way.

Once we reached our car and placed our luggage in the perfect size trunk, and were seated and ready to go, we dug out of our carry-on a critical guest, Earl. Earl was also known as our navigator for the next few weeks. Back in the United States, we preloaded Earl with all our European maps and hotel addresses.

My wife plugged in destination number one: Stresa, Italy. A few seconds later Earl directed us to head south to get on the A1. Following these directions, we drove for a few short kilometers before entering the A1. It was raining as we left the airport and metropolitan Zurich.

Just minutes after entering the A1, the awesomeness of the Alps appeared in the distance. Although the rain was pounding down on our car, their form translated loud and clear.

The stimulating Swiss Alps were all around us, a site I had been waiting to see for several months. Even looking through the somewhat foggy windows, the sheer magnitude of the Alps made their impact on all of us in the car. Holy cow!

Thinking about how I was feeling at that moment, my thoughts pointed to the direct correlation between travel and performing on stage from week to week. Perhaps my grogginess was turning into something positive. My inner sense of longing began to wake up.

I started to understand my love for Europe, as well as my emotional attachment to performing on stage. My desire to live, experience, and perhaps become one with the continent became apparent as did my recollection of the years of past performances of my own here in Europe.

At this time, I was unaware of the full, or shall I say, real message waiting for me. Soon, all would be made clear. My instincts and desires came alive and affected me on a completely new, new level. In time, I would have a higher knowledge of not only why I adored Europe, but why I felt so connected to it.

Continuing on our journey, I began to feel the full impact of travel fatigue. I was exhausted from our seven-hour flight, that along with the six-hour time change, I was struggling to stay awake. After about an hour of driving through the mountains and in and out of tunnels, my eyelids became very heavy and my vision extremely blurry. Fearful of an accident, I pulled over at the next rest stop.

This rest stop was a simple one, used for resting and the facilities, not for food or shopping. I jumped out of the car so that I could stretch my legs. Slapping my wet hands to my face, I felt the blood begin to rush back. Feeling better, I got back into the car within about 10 minutes of stopping.

Pulling over and getting out of the car helped the circulation in my body, my legs, and my mind. The short pitstop built my confidence, and I felt I could make the remaining 200 kilometers without issue. With renewed energy, I felt I was able to continue.

Following signs toward Stresa, we continued south toward Axenstrasse on Route 2/E41. We passed a road sign indicating that Milano was 175 kilometers away, and Lugano was just 125 kilometers both towns we would ultimately visit. We were drawing nearer, and I was feeling good.

There was only one issue to note: the further south we traveled, the heavier the rainfall was. The steady downpour had a mesmerizing if not, hypnotic effect on me. With each rainy kilometer traveled, my eyelids became even heavier than before; I was struggling to hold it together.

I was hopeful that I could engage my wife or sons in some stimulating conversation, to keep me awake. To my dismay, I discovered that all were nodding off in the back seat. I knew that I was on my way to joining them, which I had to prevent. I pounded my backside in and out of the seat cushion to keep myself awake, each time affording me another two minutes of struggle-free driving.

To add to my already debilitating fatigue, we hit another tunnel, this particular one seeming endless. This specific tube reminded me of the tunnel which runs through Mont Blanc which is 11.6 kilometers. The Mont Blanc Tunnel is a tunnel linking Chamonix, France, and Courmayeur, Aosta Valley, Italy. In the belly of Mont Blanc, there were signs everywhere telling us, the drivers, to keep a strict distance between the car in front of us.

Continuing through the tunnel, I found myself entirely hypnotized by measured lights on the side of the tunnel, the ceiling tile design and dotted white lines in the middle of the road; I could not focus another minute. My eyes were dancing inside my head, and I knew I was in trouble.

I woke my wife and asked her to keep me company. I told her that I was in trouble and didn't want to fall asleep at the wheel. In her absolute supportive disposition, she opened her bag and offered me an apple or a pear; I took the pear. Eating helped and welcoming the much-needed conversation worked in conjunction to do the trick.

We talked about where we were, what we were doing, and why we had traveled so far. There is much to see, experience, and enjoy as a family. It seems that we had just begun our journey, starting at the airport in Newark and here we were staring at the Swiss Alps, through a foggy windshield.

Although neither of us thought of an airport as a romantic place, this trip made us feel differently. If you strip away the hustle and bustle of airport life and only think about the reasons why people are traveling, it can become fascinating, and we felt, even romantic.

To make the trek back home, to be reunited with their family, friends, loved ones. Were they taking an exciting trip to new and inspiring cities, countries and villages? What can be more romantic than those thoughts? Our fantasies entered the conversation as well. That was the topic of our discussion for the next hour.

During our talk, the tunnel opening appeared in the distance; it was one of the most beautiful sights I had seen in a long time.
What a relief!

As we exited the tunnel, there was another reason to wake up and become more excited; it had stopped raining. As we drove through the tunnel, we had cut through a chunk of Switzerland on our way to Italy, and the clouds had dissipated. The tunnel, carved into the mountainside, had exceptionally high elevation, cutting off the cumulonimbus clouds from the start of the tunnel all the way to the end.

We had experienced this once before on a trip from Geneva, Switzerland to Aosta, Italy and were laughing at the fact that we were living through the same experience again. Both times, we experienced the rain stopping after a long tunnel trip from Switzerland to Italy, and the irony wasn't lost on us.

Shortly thereafter, we came upon a real rest stop, one with petrol, food, and coffee. We all agreed to stop and make use of the facilities, and I for one was happy to pull over and take a much-needed break.

I glided into the waiting parking spot, and just ahead of me, I could see signs for Ascona and Locarno. Both locations are in Switzerland, just outside of the Italian border.

Once I had pulled over, I shut the car off and proceeded to the rest stop building. The only thing on my mind was coffee. I got in the queue, and a few short minutes later, had in my hands one of the best cups of espresso I ever had.

After using the facilities, I met up with my youngest son and asked if he would like to have something to eat. It took about two seconds for Daniel to decide on a spremuta d'arancia (fresh squeezed orange juice) and a slice of Margherita pizza. It took him only about 28 additional seconds for him to consume the meal.

Afterward, we headed back to the car, woke up Earl, and continued on our journey to Stresa. Earl informed us that we still had one-and-a-half hours before we would arrive at our hotel. But, looking at the amount of distance remaining, I saw it was only about 80 kilometers (48 miles) away, making me think that. I could cover that in under an hour.

The reason Earl had given what seemed like a very conservative arrival time became obvious about ten minutes later. The roadway dropped us down to 60 kilometers an hour (35 MPH), a far cry from the 120 kilometers we were cruising at before.

For the next 70 kilometers, we weaved through small towns, mostly on single lane roads. In some cases, it not only appeared to be a one lane road, but there was two-way traffic! I drove carefully in and out of this scenario while hugging the mountainside best I could.

To add to the drama of driving, I had to contend with our European friends flying by our car on their motorcycles. When I say flying, I mean *flying*. The motorcyclists would find the perfect moment to make their move, just when there was a split second to dart out from around our car as another car passed us by in the opposite direction. At the precise moment, they would hit the throttle and zoom on past. As each cyclist pulled up behind me, the more terrified I felt, not for me, but for them!

After a while of observing this, I thought to myself this was more than just driving their hogs, this was an art form, a societal must, a challenge, or better yet, a way of life.

Motorcycle after motorcycle came flying by in what I can only describe as a pompous act of passage. The more we drove, the more we experienced the flying Italians. *Zoom*, they went soaring by, sometimes two at a time. I caught myself looking into my rearview mirror more than the front windshield. The passing motorcycles added to the enjoyment of the ride, making the next hour pass quickly.

We followed the SS33 for more than 30 kilometers, making our way to Stresa. Along the way was the marvelous, glorious Lake Maggiore. I found myself pulling over from time to time for the sole reason of taking a quick snapshot of our spectacular surroundings. The view was like something out of a history book or a postcard picture.

The Ticino region of Italy is just breathtaking. As we slowed down to enter the Hotel Regina parking lot, our collective necks snapped leftward – directly across the street from the front of the hotel was the picturesque Lake Maggiore. I knew where we would be enjoying a nightcap this evening.

Losses

"For death is no more than a turning of us over
from time to eternity" ~William Penn

Diary entry: April 19, 2016 2:36 a.m.

It has been a difficult six months. The day before Thanksgiving, I said goodbye to my longtime friend Ray, who died peacefully in his sleep at the age of 93.

Ray was surrounded by his family when he joined his wife who left so many years before. I am glad that I stayed in touch with Ray and his son until his final days. He was a unique man, one who appreciated the art of writing, more specifically, pen paling. It was Ray who prompted me in the mid-1980's to keep a journal of my daily life. I shared my once in a lifetime relationship with this "stranger" from Kerrville, Texas in my first book.

It wasn't until about a year before Ray passed that I learned his actual age. I believed he was my elder by about 25 years. When I found out that Ray was 40 years older, I needed time to process this information. He always displayed such high energy and dedication towards his hobbies, collecting vintage snare drums, miniature cars replicas, and had an insatiable passion for writing, and documenting.

Years ago, he shared with me that he thought I was going to have a "fascinating career." He emphasized that if I didn't keep a written record of the events I would live through, they would go untold. I had no idea how correct his advice would turn out to be! In my current career, documenting each event of my daily work is not only important, but it is also mandatory.

I had spent the better part of 30 years hanging out with this guy via letters, (not emails but actual handwritten letters), all of which I still possess.

Ray was invested in my life and work both on and off the stage. He honestly cared about me as if I were his own, which offered a real blessing in my life. We had known each other for more than a decade before I decided in 2003, I needed to get myself to Texas to finally meet the man who had been advising me all this time.

Years later when Ray's son called me to share that Ray had passed, I paused for a moment to reflect on the greatness of this man and all he meant to me before responding. I was sorry to hear this news but knew Ray had been very sad since his wife Margie left him some years ago. Now, they are back together, and I can only imagine their happy reunion.

Just before Ray's passing, his son, Lindy shared with me, that he had brought Ray to a nursing home. Here, there would be people who could keep watch over his father, my friend. The cost was very high, and the expenses needed his attention.

Many years ago, in Ray's prime as a working professional, he owned an extensive collection of vintage snare drums, which dated from the turn of the 20th century. There were real gems in his collection, rare drums from the Leedy, Ludwig, Gladstone, and duplex companies. It was an extremely desirable collection for any serious collector to possess.

I myself, like Ray, collected vintage snare drums. I enjoyed a vast collection as well numbering over 60 at its peak.

I sometimes thought that I should ask him to sell me one or more of his most prized possessions, but always stopped myself from writing such a letter. Our relationship stems from a sincere appreciation of life and family alike, not just vintage drums.

It wasn't until years later that I learned Ray sold his collection to one dealer. Selling to one single collector awarded him maximum value for his decades of investments. In addition, he was also in the process of downsizing. I remember this period well as he shared that he sold his 6-person RV sleeper for a much smaller Aerostar camper.

When Lindy needed to put Ray into a nursing home for his safety, he emailed me the following:

Sunday, April 6, 2014, at 11:45 p.m.

"When Kerry was in Kerrville, she inventoried Ray's remaining drums. Some of the writing on the drums was hard to decipher, but this is the best we can do. 1965 Rogers Powertone, 1972 Premier "2000" Chrome 14 X 6, 1940 Slingerland (Mahogany), RM-10 Military Rope Drum 9.5 X 13.75, Jeri Marsch-und Konzert-tromMeln (NR 200), 3X15 (no name on the drum) with 1929 date and 1924 Leedy Elite "Black Beauty."

If you are interested in the drums, please make an offer (to help offset some of Ray's nursing care costs). I can make arrangements to have them shipped to you. If you're not interested, can you advise about what to do with the drums? Thanks for your consideration. Keep up the good work with your music world.

I was taken aback by Lindy's email, as I was sure Ray sold his collection years ago. Alas, I was wrong, and now, a new dialog began. I told Lindy that I would be happy to deal with selling Ray's drums, no problem. I also asked him about Ray's famous red journals.

In a March 2003 letter to Ray, I wrote the following:

"I have a story to share with you. Many years ago, you sent me a photograph of all your famous "red" journals—volumes and volumes. The direct result of seeing that picture and reading your words to me, 'Jim, you should keep a journal and write about all events and gigs,' is that I have kept a thorough journal all these years. All because of that great picture you shared with me."

Over the next months, Lindy and I exchanged emails several times, the first one being just two days after receiving Ray's drums. I had sold two of the most expensive instruments and needed to know where to send the money.

To: wieb@gmail.com
From: Jim@JimNeglia.com
Saturday, May 24, 2014, 10:43 a.m.

"The drums and journals arrived earlier this morning. I am in the thick of sorting through all the boxes. I am taking pictures of the drums so I can put them online and am also researching prices for each instrument. Everything arrived undamaged.

I am overwhelmed, moved, and downright emotional during the unpacking process. I remember seeing all of these drums during my visit years ago to Ray's home. The memories came flooding back with each box I opened. A fantastic reason to smile today, first for having the trust of my dear friend's family, as well as the chance to help during this, the ending process."

June turned into July, and subsequently, August. Most of Ray's items were now in new homes with people who can appreciate their value."

Friday, November 28, 2014, at 2:48 p.m.
"Kerry, Maddie and I are in Kerrville with Ray this week. Ray has his good days and his bad days. When he's having a good day, he remembers you and asks us to say hi. I'll make sure we tell him hello for you. There's no

change in his health or memory since we last visited in October and we hope to have many more days with him.

Kerry's been busy going through Ray's belongings to get them ready to sell. She found a lot of miscellaneous drum items of interest that you may like: two scrapbooks with various pictures, several old drum catalogs, books, drumsticks, drum heads, and a lot of other knick knacks, including a couple of letters from you.

We put them in the mail to you today; I hope that's fine. If some items have value, could you let me know? Other things may be of sentimental value, and you can keep, sell, or give them away as you like.

Again, we appreciate all you're doing for Ray. Have a Merry Christmas."

Saturday, November 29, 2014, at 1:41 a.m.
"I am pleased to hear Ray is holding his own, that makes me very happy. I am equally delighted to hear that when he is having a good day, he remembers me. I understand that all his days may not be the best, but when I hear he has some memory of days gone by, that brings a smile to my face. Thank you for sharing this with me.

I am humbled and honored that you and Kerry are sending me more of Ray's belongings, those that I am sure he enjoyed. I assure you, if there are items of value, I will sell them and get you the receipts right away. I am deeply touched that both of you decided to include me in part of the process.

I am so happy to think that you have unearthed some of Ray's letters to me! I am very much looking forward to the package.

I trust you and your family had a wonderful Thanksgiving. As holidays like this pass, they serve as a reminder of just how fortunate we all are. I, for one, am thankful for your friendship, trust, and understanding. It means so very much to me to have your support."

Saturday, November 29, 2014, at 2:49 p.m.
"Your note brought shivers to Kerry and me, much appreciated. The package was sent at book rate, so it might be a while before arriving. Let me know when the box of drum equipment arrives; I'm anxious to hear about it. Again, thanks for all you're doing for us and for the kind words."

Wednesday, December 3, 2014, at 11:52 a.m.
"The package arrived. As I opened it, I nearly began to cry tears of love, memories, and even some old letters. I have not opened the photo albums yet, as I need to wait until I have some uninterrupted downtime to enjoy the entire box. I am very grateful to you and Kerry for trusting me with these items. I am without words."

Friday, December 5, 2014, at 12:11 p.m.
"There was any number of items in the magical box that you and Kerry were kind enough to send me. Among the absolute treats were many of my letters to Ray. I have all of the ones he wrote to me, and now, I can add them to the letters I sent to Ray all those years ago.

I have also learned that he had many friends, more letters, some of which I read with great enthusiasm. Ray was always sincere with me, and now, I see he was this warm to everyone he was in contact. What an exceptional man. His sticks, brushes, drum head, and drum keys are all priceless gems to me. I will cherish them always.

One of the most fantastic finds was the articles which Ray had published in "Not So Modern Drummer" magazine. The real kicker for me is that all of his original correspondences with the magazine are in the box. All of the articles he wrote as a proposal for publication are all handwritten, no typewriter required. To top it off, there was a letter from the publication upon them accepted his articles. In the box were all the offers Ray submitted, letters of acknowledgment from the magazine, as well as the actual magazine itself.

Ray is a meticulously detailed person; I knew that by his journal alone, but now I see even more evidence of his busy pen. I am honored to have these items in my home. It is a priceless collection of one man's desire to share with others, and his vast knowledge of the vintage drum world.

I am blessed to have crossed paths with Ray, Margie, you and your lovely family. I will continue to push the remaining drums I have here in New Jersey and forward, whatever comes from them. I am grateful for your trust and friendship, a constant reminder of what is good in life."

Friday, December 5, 2014, at 12:28 p.m.
"You've made our day! Not knowing what to do with many of Ray's items, we're so happy to have found a home for his drum collection. We are grateful that you not only accepted his items but discovered personal value in them.

We'll keep you updated on Ray's condition. Thanks for the beautiful note."

In late January 2015, Lindy shared with me that Ray has pneumonia and Hospices have been brought in. They are taking things day by day. I shared with Lindy my concern and support. He responded via email:

Monday, January 19, 2015, at 7:56 p.m.
"There's not much the doctors can do for Ray's pneumonia, but his vitals are good. He's comfortable and has lucid moments where we can carry on conversions. Hospice said there's no way to tell how long Ray has left. Kerry and I are staying in Kerrville, perhaps for the duration.

There's nothing you can do outside of thoughts and prayers. I'm happy that you were gracious with Ray's drums and personal items. I know Ray would be grateful that you're thinking of him. I'll certainly keep you informed of Ray's progress. Thanks for caring."

Monday, January 19, 2015, at 9:56 p.m.
Although it is what I expected to hear, I am still sad to hear the news. I know that Ray has lived a long life, filled with loving family and friends. He gave of his time, always with kindness and genuine concern. It is a blessing that our paths crossed all those years ago and that we were able to continue our friendship to this day. I am proud to have included him

in my book, a place where his memory will live on in thought and words for all who read.

It sounds like he is resting without pain. My only wish is that Ray does not suffer, but will fall into a deep sleep, awakening to the sight of Margie with open arms."

Journal Entry: Sunday, January 25, 2015, 10:46 p.m.
I have several friends who are either in their 90's or approaching the ninth decade of life. Since Ray's decline, I have called each of them just to let them know how much of an impact they have had on my life.

Sunday, February 1, 2015, at 2:39 p.m.
"Ray seems to be improving after what looked like a steep decline. He's getting his strength back. Yesterday, he was entirely alert, telling us stories of his life and making jokes about dating the girls around the facility. I asked him if he remembered you and he absolutely did, Margie, too."

Roughly nine months later, Ray began his final decline. Life was coming full circle.

Tuesday, November 24, 2015, at 3:06 p.m.
"Jim, Ray passed away this morning in his sleep. Kerry and I were fortunate to be by his side and blessed that he was at peace at the end. His service is tomorrow, 2 p.m., in Kerrville, so keep Ray in your thoughts and prayers at that time. Thanks for being such a good pen pal."

When I received Ray's drums, they all had tags, with one side of the label holding a short description of the drum and on the other, who he would bequeath the instrument too.

The drums that were labeled were not the most expensive nor desirable instruments in his collection but held some intrinsic value.

Ray's Tags

I came across a note from Ray, dated January 4, 2010, which was the last hand-written correspondence I would ever receive from my nearly three-decade pen pal.

January 4, 2010

Dear Jim,
So glad to hear from you. You're still my favorite pen pal. I'm now living alone, as Margie passed on June 11. I'm adjusting; I went to five bereavement classes that helped me a great deal. There is a possibility that I may move to Colorado to be near my daughter. Hope you are well and making a lot of music.

As Ever,
Ray

You Do What?

"Do not argue with an idiot. He will drag you down to his level and beat you with experience." ~Anonymous

It is my passion to work with others, to enable them to perform at their highest possible level attainable each day. I feel a lot of that has to do with providing a professional, stress-free environment for my colleagues. Sounds simple, no?

In all honesty, it is an extremely challenging task, one that requires my complete, undivided attention. It's a task I have devoted my life's ambition too.

Each day when I arrive at work, whether it be at the Symphony, or a freelance event, my approach is identical. I enter at the appointed place and time with a smile on my face. I walk in with a bounce in my step. One would be surprised how infectious this approach can be. I believe that positive energy is entirely transferrable and will enter others through their subconscious, even if they aren't aware.

On the off chance that I am having a bad day, conversely, it is instantly felt by most, if not all, of the personnel. I do my best to stay away from those negative feelings, but I am human and suffer just like the rest. The unfortunate side of what I do is that a person in my position does not have the option of a *bad day*, ever.

A personnel manager's job description throughout the industry looks something like this:

- Proven, effective and efficient written and oral communications skills.
- Knowledge and experience with electronic media and their associated American Federation of Musician agreements.
- Superior organizational skills and the ability to schedule priorities to maximize efficiency and institutional goals.
- Ability to work under pressure, with a wide variety of personalities while exhibiting patience, understanding, and a sense of humor.
- Knowledge of symphonic repertoire.
- Familiarity with orchestra industry practices, traditions, and a working knowledge of musicians collective bargaining agreement.

Administrative Duties:

- Create and maintain a musician contact list.
- Manage musician payroll.
- Maintain substitute musician lists as prescribed by principals and the Music Director.
- Hire substitute musicians, as needed.
- Produce weekly rosters for the Librarian and Production Manager.
- Track musician service counts.
- Process musicians leave requests.
- Track all musician leave days used, roll over any unused days.
- Keep local chapter of the American Federation of Musicians updated on contracts and musician violations.
- Help obtain O-1 visas for foreign musicians.
- Maintain musician personnel files.
- Keep time for rehearsals and performances, in conjunction with the stage manager.

Concert/Rehearsal Duties:

- Attend all services.
- Take attendance.
- Act as official timekeeper.
- Ensure compliance with the Collective Bargaining Agreement.
- Inform guest conductors of rehearsal practices.

Other:

- Arrange and attend tenure-track meetings with Music Director and probationary musicians.
- Create and maintain a list of ensembles for hire.
- Attend all Staff and Production Meetings.
- Keep the General Manager informed of all aspects of the position.
- Perform other duties as needed.

My favorite part of the description is the final point listed "Performs other duties as needed." The understanding of the word *'other'* is derived only from years of experience, as one never knows what else will come up during the day. The job description is just the tip of the iceberg of what our real duties encompass.

For those of us who are playing personnel managers (meaning musicians who perform by playing an instrument with the orchestra), it adds a layer to the mix. While wearing both hats, we must keep in mind that at all times we have no, that is zero leeway with lack of focus or screwing up. Just because we are performing, it does not allow any flexibility in our personnel manager duties, performing is secondary in all cases.

Over the years, I have come to understand the most challenging aspect of my personnel manager position is that of perception. Regardless of how I act, how much I care, how I handle isolated issues, my ultimate judgment comes with how my actions are perceived. Perception is always problematic by the fact that we will never, ever satisfy the entire membership on any given topic. That is just part of our lives as orchestra personnel managers.

It is always quite telling when I revisit my contemporaneous notes on my players. It is through this process that I may see if I acted appropriately, or if I could have offered an alternate solution. In all cases, I learn and grow.

I am thought of by some as their therapist, their confidante, their advisor, their mentor, or even their friend. When a player shares with me intimate details of their life, in return, I show concern by offering them my understanding and support. I enjoy a great satisfaction when I can help my players resolve an issue, whether professional or personal.

Another aspect of my job that is difficult to deal with is when musicians feel that I am their opposition. This negative mentality comes to pass because I am considered part of management. In our industry, there is a myth that management and membership cannot coexist peacefully. Many musicians feel the administration is always trying to get something over on them.

I do my best to smooth out those rising feelings and potential problems before the tension peaks. I have always felt for those who subscribe to this way of thinking, feeling compassion for their shallow perspective. Yet, I do empathize with where the sentiment hails.

When both sides are transparent in their approach to resolve an issue, only then can there be a chance for a successful outcome. If successful, the healing begins, and our ensemble once again becomes a healthy, functioning organism.

Issues can develop over the simplest of problems, as anyone who has been a working professional can probably imagine. Take the topic of musician seating within the orchestra. In the string section, seating takes on an additional meaning, since often those on the violin, viola, cello, and bass sit two people per music stand. This can cause discord due to, the vision of a stand partner, the site line to the conductor, or lack of respect for your stand partner. To further complicate matters, the person on the right might be playing a different part of the music than the musician on the left of the same music stand. When playing two separate parts by the pair of stand partners, we call this musical term, divisi. When divisi is employed, I am more in tune with the problems caused by disrupting a current seating structure.

Sometimes, a string player is asked to change their seating because another player has called in sick and the sick player was sitting ahead of the requested player. In all cases, I try to disrupt the section as little as possible, moving the last player in the section, the player in the back of the section on the last seat to swing forward to the newly vacant seat. Musicians must comply with that request as "move up" is part of our CBA.

Try to imagine you have practiced a particular part, and when you walk into work, you find that you are not sitting in the seat the corresponds to the divisi part you have prepared. In cases like this, I forgo the CBA because a real concern comes into play. This and overshadows the language outlined in our bylaws, that of the artistic integrity.

Over the years, the musicians learn that I have a complete understanding of this complexity and have confidence I will look out for them. This awareness of my sensitivities removes anxiety from the player and section as a whole, creating an environment that is conducive to unimpeded performance.

These illustrations are just the tip of the iceberg of the issues I deal with on a regular basis. There are so many stories, it makes me think that I could complete my trilogy on a sequel on this very topic.

What is a CBA?

"It's not wise to violate rules until you know how to observe them."
~T. S. Eliot

A collective bargaining agreement (CBA) is a particular type of commercial agreement, usually one that's negotiated "collectively" between management and trade unions. The collective agreement regulates the terms and conditions of employees in the workplace, their duties as employees, as well as the duties of the employer. The CBA contains everything from membership duties to compensation, scheduling to obligations of each party, physical working conditions are spelled out, engagement of personnel (both temporary and long-term), termination process, grievances, benefits, electronic media clauses as well as committees of the orchestra, standard of conduct, and much more.

A CBA is vital to all organizations as it lays out the "do's and don'ts," of their daily operations. My duties as a personal manager include completely and thoroughly upholding the letter of the CBA, regardless of the human aspect of a given issue.

I have experienced in my career, the language that is outlined in the CBA in theory, sometimes, doesn't work in application. If an article works against a musician, I reach out to the orchestra committee chair and explain to them why the article doesn't work or apply to the given situation. If it works against management, I operate in the same way with my superiors.

Yet other times, I am compelled to support issues that are unclear in our CBA. Such support can put me in the position of defending our musicians or management. Talk about problematic sides!

I work for our players, but am paid by the administration. Therefore, it is my job to piece the issue together from start to finish. These difficulties illustrate just some of the difficult positions that I am placed in regularly.

A CBA is voted on by the membership and includes its terms and length of the agreement. We have had two-year deals, as well as three or even four-year contracts in the past. No matter how long I have been doing my job, I learn something new every single season. Each time the language does not correspond to the practice required for a particular circumstance, I make a note of it. When the time is right, I show my notes to my superiors. I also share them with the musician's committee, who will be negotiating new language for the next CBA. I point out to both parties how the language does not work and why.

Although I make my presentation on an entirely bipartisan level, there are those on both sides who may question if I, the personnel manager, may have particular motivations. I do understand those who think this way; it is healthy, almost natural. However, I can tell you with complete honesty that my motivation is to demonstrate complete transparency. This approach benefits both the membership and management, as it allows me to gain the trust of each party, as well as build positive relations for future negotiations.

One year, long after we held auditions for assistant principal viola, it was clear we needed to make some severe changes in our antiquated audition procedure.

When administering auditions, the CBA requires the membership to vote on a committee who adjudicates the applicants. It also requires me to hire a staff who works behind the scenes, assisting the applicants. These are musicians who sign in each candidate: they take each candidate to their warm-up room, keep track of where each applicant is, assign them a number for auditioning, and ultimately, help all candidates onto the stage for their actual audition.

One member of the committee, another member of the backstage staff, as well as myself, got together after the auditions were long over to chat about how we could make the process smoother. We all knew we avoided many potholes in the audition process and that the current language we were bound to follow no longer worked. The three of us agreed to a communal powwow to address this.

During our unified meeting, we quickly decided that the language in place for the past few decades needed an update. After a few hours of dissecting each part of the article, we came to a consensus.

When the other two members presented the changes to the orchestra and shared why they were necessary, there was little to no pushback from the membership. Shortly after sharing the changes with them, a vote took place. The vote passed overwhelmingly to present the new language to the management, and ultimately, made its way into the next CBA.

I attribute the success of the passage partially to my lack of recognition during the process. Instead, members of the orchestra showed support for each other, as there appeared to be no interference from management. I was perfectly fine going without praise, as the changes serve the organization as a whole and will benefit the membership for years to come.

This offers a small example of my duties within our organization, my responsibilities to the players, and my desire to always do the right thing. I can only hope that my legacy will be based in upholding the integrity of the organization as an entirely viable entity.

> "Never argue with an idiot. They will drag you down to
> their level and beat you with experience." Mark Twain

Years ago, I witnessed a particular player box themselves into a corner. I caught this said player using their handheld device during a rehearsal, causing them to miss entrance after entrance. When rehearsal was over, I spoke to the musician directly, informing them that they could only use their device during breaks.

I stated "I understand you may have wished to learn the translation of some of Mahler's markings, but in doing so, you were missing entrances. In the future, should you have questions, feel free to ask your section principal. Or, in the case of this series, our German speaking guest conductor.

As a member of the Artistic Advisory Committee, I am sure you understand how inappropriate it is to use such devices during rehearsals or performances."

They responded:

"Actually, I speak German at a high, almost fluent level— "unbelievably high" in the exact words of our guest conductor. If with the five or six unfamiliar words I discreetly looked up on my iPhone dictionary in the course of four rehearsals I was late on an entrance or two, it would be no different from the other ways we take action in service of the music during rehearsals, such as coordinating bowings, and divisi.

Just to make sure that the conductor did not feel offended if he happened to catch a glimpse of me doing this, and perhaps mistake it for text messaging or emailing, I made it a point to speak with him about it at the first rehearsal, at which time he expressed no problem whatsoever with me.

To the contrary, at the conclusion of the first concert, he congratulated me individually on my performance. Most people tend to plod through a Mahler score without knowing precisely what all the markings mean - my actions were a reflection of my desire to refine my level of contribution, based on the most precise understandings of markings I may not have noticed before. I do disagree that my actions were somehow inappropriate but I can understand from your point of view how it would be impossible for you to know the difference between what I was doing and the droves of others who text during rehearsals, so I will refrain from using the PDA dictionary in the future during rehearsal time."

You may ask, how does one respond to such a level of nonsense? This phone call demonstrates a treasure trove of convoluted, defensive, egoistic garbage.

Final discussion …
"The question is not how well you speak German, nor is it pertinent to this discussion. The issue here is the usage of your iPhone during rehearsal.

Guest conductors have no idea about our policies; only personal managers know what is permitted and what is not. Stated on Page 32 of our musicians' handbook, cell phones, and handheld devices are not allowed on stage/in wings at any time. So, I beg to differ that using a PDA for a translation isn't synonymous with coordinating bowings, and divisi. I suggest looking at your dictionary before the rehearsal to gain a complete understanding of the score. Another possibility could have been to check the translations on the 20-minute break, provided at all four rehearsals. Another option would be to ask our capable concertmaster or guest conductor. All possibilities.

Personally, I have no "view" regarding texting, translations, word searches, phone calls, etc. This is policy brought forth by you and your colleagues. My job and sole objective in this matter is to enforce the rules of your CBA and nothing more.

The comments I made to you yesterday were at the tuning, not before. Regardless, please review Page 32 of the musicians' handbook for clarification. I consider this matter closed."

My suggestion to all players of all orchestras, don't push the personnel manager, they will have the goods and can produce them at a moment's notice!

Ticino Region

"The world is a book and those who do not travel read only one page."
~Augustine of Hippo

August 10 – day 3, 50 Kilometers
Ascona, Verbania, Monte Brè and Locarno

After enjoying a most delicious filling breakfast of espresso, eggs, cheese, hams, yogurts, fruits, granola, and assorted juices, we headed out. We hopped on the SS33 and drove north on our 53-kilometer journey to the charming city of Ascona.

Geographically, Ascona is only about 50 kilometers from Stresa, but those 30 miles would take us more than an hour to travel.

On the seemingly single-lane, two-way traffic continued for the foreseeable future, I clutched the wheel and proceeded as carefully as the road and drivers would allow. We were forced to slow down and speed up as dictated by the winding road, rather than a set speed limit. Once again, the motorcycles were in complete command over each inch of the road, passing cars at blinding speeds. I am now convinced this method of driving is necessary for them to uphold their position on the course.

Roughly 16 kilometers into the trip, we came to a sudden and unexpected halt. We weren't moving at all, standing idle, the car engine shut down from the built-in mechanism on the hybrid model we had rented.

While we were waiting on the highway parking lot, we began to rethink our plans. Should we turn around and instead visit some other town along the Lake? During our debate, the traffic started to move forward ever so slightly. A few minutes later, we saw in the distance on our left, the small town of Verbania.

As we approached the roundabout, we could see that there were tents set up as far as the eye could see. The decision to stop was a no-brainer. What we didn't know was that the traffic had come to the sudden stop due to an enormous open market and festival atmosphere in Verbania itself.

I pulled off the roundabout into the public parking area. After circling a few times, we were fortunate to find a spot which was being vacated by a content market attendee. After putting money into the meter box and placing the ticket receipt on our dashboard, we headed into the small town.

Here, we found endless blocks of market stands, all covered from the sun by the shelter of their tent tops. There was an unending labyrinth of stands, one more enjoyable than the next. We came across stands filled with leather goods, wooden toys, sundresses, shorts, and skirts. Towards the back of the tented area, there were mountains of food choices. So many, you could find any possible food your imagination could dream up. There were samples of dozens of salamis, cheeses, fish, meats, and fruits that melted in your mouth. There were rows upon rows of the most succulent peaches, plums, figs, blood oranges, apples and grapes ever witnessed by this traveler, all for the taking, or purchasing. We spent a few hours milling about, enjoying our surroundings.

I always found that some of the best times we have ever had while visiting Europe were whenever we stumbled onto an unexpected market When this happened, we have never, ever been disappointed.

With full bellies, we got back in the car and proceeded north on the SS33 towards Ascona, hugging the shore of Lake Maggiore. We had only 40 kilometers to travel before hitting the Ascona city limits. Once parked, we made our way down to the lake area.

Ascona is known for its Mediterranean-style architecture and cafe-lined promenade on Lake Maggiore. In the old town of Borgo, there is the 16th-century Church of St. Peter and Paul. There is also the Museum of Modern Art, both of which are worth a visit.

Regardless of what Ascona is known for, what was most present before our eyes were the number of Gelaterias! They are in view as far as the eye could see. My son Daniel was in his glory! Strawberry, vanilla, chocolate, pistachio, lemon, and fifty more varieties all waiting for our consumption, which we happily obliged. Taking some refuge from the hot sun under the shade of the trees, we enjoyed the view of the Lake while savoring the coolness of our cones.

On our drive to Ascona, we noticed that Locarno was nearby and decided to add it to our return agenda. After a few hours of exploring in Ascona, we headed off to see what Locarno had to offer. While driving towards Locarno, W we came to a juncture in the road. To the right, would bring us to the downtown area of Locarno. However, if we headed to the left, the roadway would take us to the curious area of Monte Brè. What now! There was much desire to explore the area of Monte Brè, so westward we went!

As we began our 1500 meter drive up the incredibly narrow roadway towards Monte Brè, we quickly understood the effect of the extreme altitude of the mountain before us. Without exaggeration, we were on a single lane, two-way roadway. How is this possible? We were about to find out. The road was at best dangerous, and at worst, downright insane. If a car came into sight in the clearance ahead of us and there wasn't enough room for two vehicles to pass, someone would have to retreat into a small depression in the mountain to make way for the other passing vehicle.

The real issue was if you were the car on the outside of the road, there were no guardrails protecting you from falling down the cliff side. Driving on this roadway was downright suicidal. My dear wife was not at all happy with the roadway situation and begged me to turn around and go back. I agreed, but soon realized, that there was no possible place to make a "K" turn in order to descend the mountain, so upwards we continued.

The drive was slow going, never getting past second gear the entire trip. The road turned tightly every 30 or 40 feet, and there was no way to anticipate what was coming in front of you until it was already in sight. It was at this point that I was becoming nervous about continuing upwards and later having to make the trip back down the mountain.

Continuing up the mountain, still, in search of a safe turnaround point, we found ourselves nearly at the top. As if we hadn't experienced all we need to experience during our harrowing journey up the hill, houses started popping up out of nowhere. We began to see houses, actual homes. How can this be? Who could live up here and how, in God's good name could they possibly deal with the incredibly difficult commute?

Their location made me think of the motorcycles on the A1, the ones who drove the way they did because of societal rights. Did people live up here because they are merely permitted? No, I suspect that the homes were grandfathered in from generation to generation. The inhabitants lived there because it was no different to them if they lived at the base of the mountain range or burrowed on the side of a treacherous incline. I first need to understand the concept of entertaining the possibility of that sort of existence before continuing, but for the natives, it was the same as living on Main Street, USA.

Driving as far as we could, we came upon a road sign which had a line through the word "Road." That sign told us that we had reached the end of the public road and that anything beyond that point was private property.

I suggested we get out of the car to take some photographs in order to commemorate our journey. As I heard the clicking of the cameras, I personally took a different sort of photograph; I snapped a memory of the crisp, fresh, thin air which will forever be locked into my memory.

I sat with mouth agape taking in the scenery before us. There was nature all around, fresh air, soaring altitudes, and astonishing views. I recall thinking to myself at that very moment, "There is a God, for sure. For nothing else could create such magnificent beauty." Nature and natural wonder engulfed me like a wildfire speeding through the dry bush. We sat in silent awe for nearly 30 minutes.

Descending the mountain proved to be an easier task then the ascent with one exception— I was fearful of blowing out the breaks on our rented car.

The balance between a slow pump of the breaks along with the helpful lower gears proved to be just what we needed for a safe arrival at the bottom of the mountain. Once we arrived, we noticed that we were at the same intersection where we started our initial ascent.

I looked up only to read the sign that stood before us which read "Locarno." A few seconds later, the chimes rang out telling us it was 5 o'clock. Let's go!

As we made our way down toward Locarno, we stumbled upon a magnificent view of the Sanctuary of the Madonna del Sasso. At that time, we did not know what we were seeing, but none of us could take our eyes off of the church. Like so many vacations before, we all looked at each other with the same thought: we should park our car and do some discovering on foot.

After making a quick U-turn, we found a small parking lot and took advantage of the first vacant spot. Then, we headed down toward the Sanctuary.

The Madonna del Sasso is a sanctuary in Orselina actually above the city of Locarno. The founding of the shrine goes back to a vision of the Virgin Mary that a Franciscan brother Bartolomeo d'Ivrea experienced on a night back in 1480. There's no denying the historical significance of the place, that's for sure.

We took a very long, stone staircase down to the sanctuary, which had what seemed to be hundreds of steps, that led to the base of the shrine.

Upon entering the magnificent building, it is notable that the church was home to fantastic artwork from the 15th Century. Breathtaking architecture, woodwork, reliefs, statues, marble, and artwork surrounded us. Just to the right of the main altar, there was an area where one could light a candle in the memory of a loved one. I lit one for my brother John who left us in 2010.

We spent a good deal of time absorbing the artwork in the church, as well as a great courtyard overlooking the lake. After taking in the scenery, as well as the architectural beauty, the beautiful reliefs, and superb artwork, we decided to move on. As we were leaving the church, we saw a sign for a funicular. The sign and possible journey peaked our interest. We decided to take the funicular to wherever it would take us.

Most of the people who were on the funicular knew both the cost and destination. Since we didn't have prepaid tickets, we were fortunate to learn that we were able to pay the conductor for both andare e tornare (going and return tickets), which would lead us into the lovely heart of Locarno.

The excitement of the city was entirely unexpected. As we turned right, just outside the funicular station, we couldn't help but take in the scene before us. In the main square was an enormous screen for showing movies, amongst the largest I had ever seen in my life.

We strolled about and soaked in the cobblestone streets, the thousands of chairs set up to watch the evening's movie presentation as well as the faces surrounding us. People were walking around, enjoying the weather, sitting at full outdoor cafes, which all contributed to the feeling of mellowness the small city exuded.

Down the block from the Piazza Grande was the entrance to Parco della Pace. Once in the park, I saw dozens of free-standing tents, filled with people selling food. Not just any food, but vendors selling food from their native countries. Holy cow, what a day, what a find!

As we walked around the park, we noticed that every country's menu was on display: Indonesian, Thai, Bali, Taiwan, Italian, Vietnam, Switzerland,

France, you name it, and you could find it. We were unable to decide on what to eat, so we chose to walk around more and gaze at each offering in its preparation. By the time we left the park, we had tried every sample imaginable.

Without a purchase, we walked back to the center of the Piazza Grande, then to the left and up to the top of the mountain via the waiting, paid-for funicular, which took us up the cliff to our awaiting car.

Once in our car, we woke Earl and headed home. A short time later, we arrived at our sanctuary in Stresa, where we sipped drinks, munched on collected delectables, and made conversation. So, concludes day 3.

Chuck

Charles Kaufman

"Death is not extinguishing the light; it is only putting out the lamp because the dawn has come." ~Rabindranath Tagore

On March 17, 2016, I suffered a most devastating loss; I said goodbye to my conservatory teacher, my mentor, friend, advisor, and surrogate father; Chuck Kaufman.

Upon hearing of Chuck's passing, I sank hard into the depths of my soul with sadness. I knew that he could not live forever, but I felt he had many more years to go.

That sinking feeling was relentless and persistent. I kept asking myself, "How could this be true? How could he have left me alone?" It took hours before I began making calls to friends, in search of comfort.

The outpouring of love and affection on social media only further contributed to my overwhelming feeling of loneliness. At the same time though, a certain comfort began to take hold. I wasn't alone in my misery, and others were feeling the same abandonment, loss, and emptiness that I was.

I have often thought that I was his best friend in the entire world but later learned that most, if not all of my classmates had, thought the same. That was his miracle, his offering. When I look back at our email correspondences, I can see my entire adult life before my eyes. What a fantastic individual, what an amazingly caring person – a gift to all who were touched by the goodness, the affection, the fathering, the unconditional understanding and love of Chuck Kaufman.

That day, I posted on his Facebook page:
"I lost my dearest most valued companion imaginable. My father, my inspiration has left this universe – I believe that Chuck Kaufman has been released into all of us, his Mannes children. How I miss him, hold him close. Bless you, my dearest friend - I shall never be without you."

The text used in Mahler Symphony No. 2, titled "Resurrection" was written by the German poet Friedrich Gottlieb Klopstock. I left part of the fifth movement text on Chuck's Facebook page.

> "Rise again, yes, rise again
> Will you My dust,
> After a brief rest!
> Immortal life! Immortal life
> Will He who called you, give you.

> To bloom again were you sown!
> The Lord of the harvest goes
> And gathers in, like sheaves
> Us together, who died."

The memorial service for Chuck took place on October 7, 2016, and I had agreed to be one of the guest speakers. I was asked to prepare remarks that would last for eight to ten minutes. I could speak for days about the man of honor. A few precious minutes to share with the gathering was hardly enough to explain what he meant to me.

It was at that moment when I realized I didn't need to share my personal views. Instead, I could, or should express the views of the entire student body.

I sat down at my desk, put Mahler on my Bose system, and began to prepare for my presentation at the memorial. I was able to write an abundance of material, all worthy of sharing but somehow, it didn't seem to be complete. Something was lacking, something was missing, but I couldn't place my finger on what it was.

At a standstill, I decided to call it a night. I knew a good night's sleep would help me to bring other thoughts, other options, perhaps the truth to the forefront of my writing.

In the morning, I was eager to get back to work. While reading through my notes from the previous evening, a light bulb illuminated over my head.

My thoughts were racing with creativity. Change the "me" to "we" and "my" to "our" remember, it is not about me, but it is all about us, Chuck's Mannes family. In addition to this revelation, I decided to include a more personal side of Chuck, a side that most who went to Mannes would understand.

I settled on the last offering just a few days before the memorial. I read and reread the speech at least 20 times in preparation. I am a darn good orchestra personnel manager but wasn't sure how I would fair in my public speaking debut.

On the day of the memorial, I met with the Dean, as well as others who were part of the governing staff of the College.

Along with those who were working behind the scenes to put the memorial together, At the memorial, I was reunited with some friends I had not seen since our Master's graduation day in 1987. Here it was, nearly 30 years later, and we picked up seemingly right where we left off.

At the memorial, there were tributes in the form of speeches, musical offerings, videos, and personal reflections. My presentation was to come close to the end of the service. I have been performing all my life, in most cases in front of thousands of people each week, never to falter. But here, at this memorial, I was set to speak, not play.

On March 23, 2016, I woke up to read the following text:
"I'm sure you've heard by now. I am in shock … this is such a painful loss." I instantly knew what had happened. I Googled Chuck's name and read the *New York Times* obituary. Afterward, I spent time, silent time, reflecting on my friends passing.

When the memorial was announced, it appeared my professional obligations would prevent me from attending. Thus, I struggled to hit send on the prepared email to his son, Jason, with whom I shared my disappointment.

Jason,
Our dear Chuck, our President, our adviser, my mentor, and without pause, my surrogate father is sorely missed and respected beyond the words of this communication. I share that with you not to take him from his blood family, but to extend to you and your siblings my most profound love for this great man.

Ever since graduating in 1988, we stayed in touch. Because of his thorough knowledge as an educator, his intimate understanding as a leader, and caring guidance as a father, he was instrumental in pushing me away from potential obstacles, to a high degree of success.

I can only imagine how many others he helped in the same way. He was a remarkable visionary who was not shy about sharing his thoughts, views or input. He always spoke from his heart, even if it hurt to do so.

Chuck had made such a profound impact on my life, for which I wrote a book honoring him. In fact, Chuck was the only person I enlisted to read the raw manuscript.

He advised me, edited passages, offered input and ultimately, after a minor rewrite, blessed the final version.

I would never have sent the manuscript to my publisher without his blessing. Can you imagine anyone else taking the time to read 78,000 words and critique them?

If others relied on him as I did, you could only imagine how big his heart was. I know, without question that he was completely invested in the entire student body and treated all of us as if we were his own.

I spoke with my friend for the last time several months before his passing... although he is no longer physically here, I am confident, that we can still hear his voice in our ears through his words over the years. I distinctly remember "What do you cretins want?!?!" and "Maturity comes when you realize you can't do everything, be everywhere, and please everyone."

Nearly every sentence started with "Now, look..."

He often referred to the thematic material of early church music as "a hunk of chant," –unmistakably Chuck.

His unshakable response to "So boss, how are you doing?" Was "Still pawing away at the dirt." Typical of our friend.

One of my favorite sayings was "If you have talent, you won't be able to hide it under a rock, if you don't have any, it will quickly become apparent."

Back in 2010, after I had moved, he didn't have my new home phone number. Although I had set up the number to be unlisted, he was able to convince the operator to give him the new number, claiming that is was an absolute emergency and that *HE* was family.

Once gaining the number, he left me a message that said: "Neglia, you can't hide from me! You have 24 hours to respond, or else!" Can you imagine? How many received that very phone call; both literally and figuratively?

He used the same philosophy when communicating through emails. Do you know how many emails I would receive from him that simply said "So?" Those emails meant, he needed an update NOW.

Mostly, I would write to him long, very long emails, filled with details, problems, union issues, and orchestra uproars, you name it; I wrote it.

He always took the time to respond completely and thoroughly, in the most sensitive (well sometimes not so sensitive) and direct way.

On one occasion, I had asked him what he had been doing. He told me he had just painted the ceiling on the porch. I thought, "Are you nuts?" He must have been in his early 80's and still, out on a ladder, in between writing chapters of his book, painting. I was blown away but dared not reprimand the boss.

On many occasions, he shared with me stories of his family, Rhoda, his son's accomplishments, his daughter in laws, cancer, his grandkids, and so much more.

I was always honored he trusted me with his inner thoughts and his family.

I knew in my heart that his time was coming to an end… it is the normal progression of life. Yet still, I found myself deeply saddened when I learned of the inevitable.

When I heard that he passed, I was convinced that I, Jim Neglia, was his best friend in the world. Right? I mean, that is what he projected all these years.

But, as I began seeing the outpouring of personal messages on his Facebook wall, I realized that one of Chuck's greatest gifts was that he made everyone feel as if *they* were his best friend.

What a gift and what a gift he shared with all of us. He actually cared about us, our health, our welfare, our careers, our wants, and needs. Chuck was 100% invested in his students, past and present and was genuinely overjoyed when we would share stories of our accomplishments. He took pride as any father would, and we, the student body reacted by loving him all the more.

A brilliant, beautiful, and tender man filled with directness, yet subtle qualities that embraced all he touched.

Truthfully, I miss our emails, our chats, and his reminders to stay focused at all cost. His depth of concern and his level of patience was beyond the norm.

As every phone call would come to an end, I would tell him, "Thank you for taking the time to chat with me" and his response was exactly the same, time after time, "I am grateful to spend this time with you."

Sadly, all the while, I didn't know of his final ailment, as he never shared that part of his life with me.

My heart is broken, as your father, my father, our father, has left this worldly existence and moved on – moved onto a place where he can continue to watch over and guide us.

Please accept my deepest, most sincere thanks, for sharing Chuck with me, with us, for all of these years. What he offered was special, beyond the meaning of the word.

I would like to share just one passage (of hundreds) from a past email exchange:

On May 20, 2013: Chuck wrote:
When your career is over, it's good to hear that you were of some consequence to someone along the line.

I also can't tell you how impressed I am with what you have built during the last 30 years—who can believe that it has been that long? Wasn't it all last week? I can remember it all with complete clarity.

Onward and Upward,
Chuck"

Lugano

"The journey itself is my home." ~Bashō Matsuo

August 11 – Day 4, 105 Kilometers
Traveling south on the A26 toward Milan, we found ourselves on the road to beauty, and I mean real beauty. The drive is paved with the most beautiful visual stimulation one can imagine.

The drive from Stresa to Lugano took us around the southern end of Lake Maggiore, starting off on the winding road of Via per Binda and Via per Verdasco. With each twist and turn, we headed through quaint villages along the charming city of Gallarate.

Once on the A36, we saw the city of Como, to the east. Once off the A2, we navigated around a dozen or more roundabouts, carefully following the signs to Lugano. As we passed a sign for Varese, just before the border control, I knew we were just a short distance away from our destination. As we passed the empty border control booths, I asked Sasha to enter "City Center," into Earl's location bank; we continued our journey.

It was warm already, and the temperature was still climbing. By the time we parked our car, it was a steamy 33 degrees Celsius (approximately 92

Fahrenheit). We are rarely bothered by the heat but today would prove to be different.

The city lies on Lake Lugano, surrounded by the mountains of the Lugano Prealps. The city center is on the lake shore, just to the west of where the River Cassarate enters the lake. The city's waterfront forms a crescent around the bay between the Brè and San Salvatore mountains, both of which we visited.

There was beauty all around, the views of the shore and mountain sides were spectacular. Etched into the mountains were picturesque houses, seemingly placed in the most perfect, strategic locations.

Natives were milling about, walking their dogs. Although simple, these sights showcased the joys of daily life here.

We usually enjoy a simple walk around town to discover things as we move about, but this time, I had a particular goal to meet—that was to visit San Sebastian. San Salvatore offers a magnificent 360-degree panorama view of the countryside below, and I had a desire to live among the clouds as this trip has thus far exceeded all my wishes.

The entrance to this site should have been about a ten-minute walk from where we were in the center of town, where a timed funicular would take us up to the pinnacle of the mountain and gateway to paradise.

All the time we were walking, the temperature continued to rise, until it felt like it was nearing 37 degrees (100 Fahrenheit). As hot as it was, there was a visible beauty just ahead of us which was in the form of large fountains with running cold water pouring out. They were placed on the road every 100 meters or so, and the water from these fountains was downright chilly, which offered a nice contrast from the hot air.

The fresh water also helped to keep our body temperatures in check and avoid overheating.

We began to see signs for Mount San Sebastian and the funicular. However, I noticed that just to the left of the funicular sign was a sign boasting the most beautiful *scenic overview*. The arrow on the sign gave the impression that the overview was just ahead of us. We all agreed to take the detour and experience the overview first-hand. This diversion proved to be a giant mistake.

Following the signs, we couldn't help but notice that the climb towards the scenic overview proved to be incredibly steep. The 5% incline quickly moved to a 15%, which made for an exhausting trip in the unmanageable heat. Once we arrived at the landing of the scenic overview some four blocks away, the arrows pointed to a set of stairs which would take us to the actual scenic overview.

So, we began our ascent. Each time we reached a landing, we would turn only to see another set of waiting stairs. By about 200 steps up, I had to open my shirt to avoid being victim to heat exhaustion. There was also no fountain in sight to offer any relief.

Continuing upward, we came to yet another landing and sign pointing 'this way' … not for me, no more steps! Daniel had enough energy to run ahead to see what was beyond our sightline. When he returned, he had nothing more to report but more stairs ahead.

Slowly, we began to descend the steps, down to the safety of the level street below where cold fountains filled with the water greeted us, to my relief.

The funicular was about six blocks from where we were and about a mile and a half from where our car was parked. It seemed to be an extremely far distance, considering our general condition and the recent failed climb.

Once we had a moment to regroup, we headed back towards toward San Sebastian. Within ten minutes, we arrived at the base of the mountain, to a tiny waiting kiosk. I purchased our tickets s to the top of the mountain.

Off we went; the ride up was breathtaking, filled with scenic views which one might only see in a Norman Rockwell painting.

Once at the top of the mountain, the earlier walk up those painful steps was now a distant memory. The emotion we felt in our new surroundings was beyond words and the exhilaration of standing in the clouds was unparalleled with anything we had experienced before.

The summit was set up with a small restaurant and Museo de San Sebastian. We visited the small museum and found letters from the 1640 and 1650, historical documents, old relics. These had a profound impact on me, since I am an avid collector of classical composer's letters, notes, visiting cards, and signed photographs.

We remained on top of the mountain for about an hour. The rolling hills, endless mountain chains, 17th Century relics, and breathtaking atmosphere all remained lodged deeply into my memory bank. Filled with the marvel which we just witnessed I could have walked 100 miles back to our car. Seven Swiss Francs later, we pulled out of the parking lot and headed back toward Stresa.

I am back in Europe for only a few days and cannot adequately describe the feeling that I am home, finally, where I belong.

Survival Mode

"A casual stroll through the lunatic asylum shows that faith
does not prove anything." ~ Friedrich Nietzsche

MARCH 2015

Monday	Tuesday	Wednesday	Thursday	Friday	Saturday	Sunday
9	10	11	12	13	14	15
FS1 & FS2 send call sheets for Carnegie 3/14 & 15	10:00 Reh **S10** Newark 1:30 Reh **S10** Newark	10:00 Rehearsal **S10** Newark 1:30 Rehearsal **S10** Newark	1:30 Perf: **S10** Newark	8:00 Perf: **S10** Newark	**FS1** 2pm-3:30 Marriott **FS2** 2pm-3:30 Sheraton 7:25 pm **S10** sound check 8:00 Perf: **S10** N.Brunswick	2:25 **S10** sound check 3:00 Perf: **S10** Morristown **FS2** 6:30 pm sound check **FS1** 7 pm sound check **FS1** 9 pm perf Carnegie Hall **FS2** 9:30 pm Perf Carnegie

16 PP15	17	18	19 Payday	20	21	22
FS3 &	10:00	10:00 Reh **S11**			**FS3** 2pm-3:30	3:00 Perf: **S11**
FS4 send	Rehearsal **S11**	Englewood	2-5	1-5 **DiMenna**	Marriott	N. Brunswick
call sheets	Englewood	1:30 Reh **S11**	**DiMenna**	Center	**FS4** 2pm-3:30	**FS3** 6:30 sd chk
Carnegie	1:30	Englewood	Center Reh	rehearsal	Sheraton	**FS4** 7 pm sd chk
3/21 & 22	Rehearsal **S11**				4-5 **DiMenna**	
	Englewood	2-5 **DiMenna**	7:30	5:25 NJSO	Center Perf	**FS4** 9 pm perf
SOPAC send		Center Reh	Perf: **S11**	bus, take it!	5:35 NJSO bus	Carnegie Hall
call sheet			Englewood		8:00 Perf: **S11**	**FS3** 9:30 pm Perf
3/25 perf				8:00 Perf: **S11**	Red Bank	Carnegie
				Princeton		
23	24	25	26	27	28	29
2-6 pm		11-5 pm	Prep for 9	9:00 am SSS	**MONTREAL→**	**MONTREAL→**
SUNY	2-6 pm **SUNY**	**SUNY**	am OPMC	**meeting**		
Recording	Recording	Recording	budget &	10:00 am		
			agenda July	OPS **meeting**		
Prepare		2:30-5:30	2016			
payroll/W9		**SOPAC**	**Confirm:**			
Forms		rehearsal	**Le Square**			
SOPAC		7:30 **SOPAC**	**Phillips**			
		Perf	**Hotel &**			
			Suites			

S10 series

Jacques Lacombe conductor - Kirill Gerstein piano
Bernstein Symphony No. 2, "The Age of Anxiety."
Mahler Symphony No. 1, "Titan."

S11 series

Jacques Lacombe, conductor - Serhiy Salov piano, Mary Fahl vocalist
Kubian *"O for a Muse of Fire"*
Rachmaninoff *"Rhapsody on a Theme of Paganini"*
Tchaikovsky *Symphony No. 6, "Pathétique"*

DiMenna Center (West 37th Street/NYC)
PROGRAM: Overture to Aida, Carmen Suite, Skaters Waltz, and Overture to William Tell

REHEARSALS:

Wednesday, March 18, 2:00 pm - 5:00 pm
Carmen, Aida and Skaters Waltz

Thursday, March 19, 2:00 pm - 5:00 pm
William Tell, Aida and Skaters Waltz

Friday, March 20, 1:00 pm - 5:00 pm
Carmen, William Tell, Aida and Skaters Waltz

CONCERT:
Saturday, March 21, 4:00 pm - 5:00 pm
Aida, Carmen, Skaters, Waltz, William Tell

SUNY Recording Sessions:
Monday, March 23 -William Tell 2:00 pm - 6:00 pm
Tuesday, March 24 - Carmen 2:00 pm - 6:00 pm
Wednesday, March 25 Aida 11:00 am - 1:00 pm
Skaters Waltz 2:00 pm - 5:00 pm

SOPAC - South Orange Performing Arts Center
The Priests! I hired the orchestra to perform with the Priests and engaged one of the musicians to act as the "on-site" contractor, in my absence. I should make it to the performance, but have a direct conflict with the rehearsal.

FS series at Carnegie Hall - (4 separate groups on back to back weekends)
For the FS3 series, I will perform as the djembe soloist, accompanying 350 voices.

During the next 19 days, I am responsible for ten S-10 services, eight S-11 services, four FS sound checks and four FS performances at Carnegie Hall, three rehearsals, one performance and four recording session for the DiMenna Center, a meeting with my boss, a meeting with the operations department, preparation of all payrolls, and travel to and from all services. I even booked a mini vacation to recuperate from the insanity, IF I survive!

If that schedule isn't enough, the real story behind the madness began when I received a phone call requesting I take over the contracting position for a high-profile New York City-based ensemble. Once the joy of the potential work sinks in, and I have had time to digest the offer, I can make an educated decision on how or if I wish to proceed. The first question I always ask when being asked to join a new organization is, "Who am I replacing and why?"

In this particular case, I knew the outgoing contractor. I also knew of the difficulties the management endured working for this particular conductor. I view the conductor as somewhat eccentric in his approach to recording music, as I had performed on one of his recordings just a few months earlier. Although the conductor may have his quirky side, that is no reason not to accept his work. However, it does add a layer of consideration to the matter.

Of course, I would not be taking the job away from the prior contractor, as the music director had already released my colleague, but it felt wrong for me to accept this work, it felt dirty.

Most contracting work pays well. This gig had the earmarks of a very well-paying series. Along with the nine hours of rehearsal and performance, there were three, four-hour recording sessions on the schedule. All services are carrying a double, if not triple, of the base rate calculated according to the local scale.

Beyond the contracting, I had already agreed to perform the services as the principal percussionist. The salary for both positions would be enough to make a severe dent in our upcoming European vacation for late August. All these factors entered my thought process when considering my decision.

While considering all aspects of the work, I glanced at the clock in my office and saw if I didn't get up at that moment, I was going to be late picking up my son from the bus stop. When it was bitterly cold outside, I always would drive up the block to the bus stop to pick up Daniel and today; it is seven degrees.

A moment after starting the car, I ran through my usual routine of connecting my iPhone to the Bluetooth mechanism. The familiar message came up on the car screen, "Would you like to connect your phone?" Although that statement appears every time I start the car, I took it as a sign to make a much-needed phone call. As I pulled out of my driveway, I dialed the outgoing contractor.

I prefaced the conversation with "This is a tough call for me to make." After explaining the offer to play and the proposal to contract, I discussed with him my hesitation to accept, due to 'taking the gig away' from my him.

The call lasted about 20 minutes and was as sincere as can be. At the end of the chat, my friend told me, "Good luck with your decision, no matter what you choose, it will be fine with me."

Despite his blessing, I was still unable to come to a firm conclusion. I knew it would be helpful if I had a night to sleep on it.

The next morning, even before making coffee, I called the music director. I started the conversation off with how honored I was to have the opportunity for the work and that I was grateful for his faith in me. I followed this with "However, I am just overwhelmed with my obligations at the Symphony and feel I can't, in good conscience, commit to this project as his contractor." I went on to share that I didn't feel comfortable giving anything less than my complete dedication to him and the project, but was grateful for the opportunity.

When I hung up the phone, I felt the weight of the world lift off of my shoulders. I texted my colleague a short but meaningful message "I just wanted to let you know, I turned the gig down. Thank you for your help, our chat yesterday, and support."

Work and money can change things between people. During my years in this business, I have witnessed the fallout between many people first hand. I, personally, have experienced this discord in my own life, too. I didn't wish for this to happen with my long-time friend and colleague and I. I know, with certainty, that turning down the position was the best decision.

The text message he sent back read "Thanks for the update; I will be calling you shortly."

A little while later, I had the following phone conversation, or shall I say, I listened attentively to the caller.

"Regardless of the outcome that you just shared with me, I was and am, sharing with you the following thoughts.

The world we live in, filled far too often with far too much cynicism (actual or perceived) and other related forces of human nature, is softened and brought into balance, when there are people such as you, who have dedicated themselves to serving others while maintaining the obvious objective of supporting themselves, families and careers.

You Jim, specifically, have done so with a most unusual ability to maintain the highest standard of integrity for yourself as a citizen of the world, but most importantly, as a kind, thoughtful, and generous human being. In this microscopic, and often overly self-indulgent profession that we have dedicated ourselves to both serving as well as benefiting, you have shown yourself the most unusual and the most esteemed standards and traits that of friendship, sympathy, empathy the willingness to consider the feelings of other people. What you possess, is in short supply.

I do not have many friends in the business, but I want you to know that regardless of where I may be in your circle, the fact that you took the time to call me on Friday and that you were considerate enough to pick up that phone and ask me for my thoughts will stand for me as a lifelong testament to who you are. With that, I hope you will always know me as a true friend to you, without limitations.

What took place over the last several days between you and me was not a test, but a confirmation! I am a very fortunate person to know you as I do and am grateful for the opportunity to be your friend and colleague."

After listening to the caller, I had a lump in my throat. I felt great, knowing I had made the right decision. Sometimes, what we perceive as a difficult decision, is something that requires an emphasis on compassion and understanding. Knowing the difference between right and wrong, while also following one's moral compass, is paramount.

After 19 straight days of intense work, I had successfully navigated through the countless gigs, bus schedules, payroll preparations, Carnegie Hall presentations, an operation meeting, and the commute from state to state and gig to gig.

I added one final item to my checklist. I booked a well-deserved mini vacation to my favorite hotel in Montreal, Le Square Phillips Hotel & Suites. Here, I would leave behind the madness of the life we live and enjoy exquisitely prepared French meals, along with the most delicious accompanying wine. Hard work is important, but celebration is also essential to leading a well-balanced existence.

Orchestra Personnel Managers' Conference

"Wisdom, compassion, and courage are the three universally recognized moral qualities of men." ~Confucius

July 27, 2013, 10:47 a.m. journal entry: Off to Edmonton

The Orchestra Personnel Managers' Conference (OPMC) is an event where personnel managers across North America gather for a three-day, intensive collaboration to discuss mutually agreed upon issues facing us in our industry.

During this sacred time, we have the opportunity to have real discussions, face to face, covering work-related issues, unresolved problems with players, unruly managers, and much more.

Here were the topics for discussion for 2017:

- Alcoholism and the orchestra
- Dealing with burnout, exhaustion, self-care
- Job re-engagement

- Tenure review procedure: who votes, what percentage of votes are needed to pass a player to the Music Director?
- Strings: substitutes players sitting with contracted members vs. substitutes sitting with only other substitutes
- The dreaded shield topic!
- Termination of personnel who get caught double dipping (calling in sick to work but performing elsewhere at the same time as our work)
- Substitute inquiries: calling us to inquire about why they aren't getting called, how to handle not being in a position to say why
- Negotiated overscale
- CBA negotiations: what kind of information/organizational financials/individual contract information do others provide to their negotiating committees before/during CBA negotiations?
- Parameters s for what constitutes an "official performance review" of a player?
- Annual meetings with individual musicians?
- Defining the "management responsibilities" of section principals? (included or not in job descriptions)
- Harassment and other workplace conflicts: does anyone use external resources or counsel? (Arbitrator, mediator, industrial-organizational psychologist, etc.)
- Rotating between violin sections – systems that work and traps to avoid?
- Using outside mediation to resolve long-standing disputes/conflict within a dysfunctional section?

It is during these precious days, where we, reconnect as a group. When we run into stressful situations, our usual procedure is to document the incident or event, and then, through various methods, find a solution. Even if there was no 'wrong '–the offended musician feels as if there was wrong and it is our position to find a way to work with the player, understand their situation from their point of view, and offer credence to the situation.

This may sound like a tall order, but we have an arsenal of tools we can implement to solve these quandaries. The resulting discussions with colleagues are remarkable, informative, relevant, as well as exciting.

The OPM group has a structure to which the body uses to house leadership, as well as facilitate communication:

-We hold elections every three years for our president, vice president, and treasurer positions.

-We record our conference minutes, which are then transcribed for group distribution.

- A closed Yahoo group (email chain) where we can share private thoughts, ask difficult questions, and gain general knowledge of the industry standard throughout North America.

During my tenure as personnel manager of the Orchestra, I have called upon my colleagues more times than I can recall.

To share one of our many exchanges, I would like to set up my circumstance. There was a substitute player whom would often come to work with a pungent scent surrounding them. We have explicit language in our collective bargaining agreement which prohibits any scented products (covering perfume, soaps, cleansers, etc.) being worn while in the workplace. Although I had spoken with the said offender on multiple occasions, the problem persisted.

A few weeks later, I was forced to have another discussion. We discussed a most recent orchestra series where I receive several complaints regarding the pungent aroma.

Although in the past I explained the steps needed for the player to comply with our no-scent policy, the problem persists. I have no alternative but to inform you if the scent issue is not resolved during the upcoming series, we will be forced to look for a different substitute player for future work.

I call several colleagues who work as personnel managers to ask their advice on my ongoing problem. Before terminating a player, I feel the need to explore every possibility to keep them on the roster.

I shared with my colleagues that we have a growing number of musicians in our orchestra who have discovered holistic oils, and that they use these oils in part to relieve stress and soothe their nerves. The problem comes from the company's stringent scent policy and holistic oils fall under that policy.

I have received numerous complaints from members, regarding the pungent odor coming from their colleagues not only on stage, but in the green room, bathroom, and hallways, as well and I have no issue enforcing our policy.

With that said, can you see any cause for concern? Are we infringing on the rights of those musicians who choose to use these oils in any way?

One of my colleagues shared that they attended a labor conference presented by the law firm of my orchestra and that they learned something very interesting. If the employer places the policy in a handbook, writes a memo which is placed in each employee's mailbox, and makes periodic announcements the employer has made a reasonable effort to make a suitable workplace environment. After that, it is up to individuals to help themselves, and from a legal standpoint, the employer cannot be held responsible.

Another colleague shouted, "WOW! Yours is the first I've seen of an official 'scent' policy!"

As to infringing upon rights, theoretically I suppose you might be, by not allowing people to use the oils, but I would think your contractual language is very clear. It is there for a reason, and that reason is to provide the best possible working environment for all of your musicians. Those that need to produce music via their breath might be most affected, but common sense needs to prevail here.

And yet another shared, that some people smoke cigarettes for the same reasons. They infringe on others, and therefore, are not allowed in the workplace.

Yet another shared with me this issue is a small example of what an orchestra personnel manager, must deal with. There is an old saying in our group which has been passed down from the older generation to the younger ones. If you're going to be in the business, there are three "D's" s, you should learn and live, as they will serve you well: document, document, and document!

Another offering from the group were their thoughts on our daily personal life and their reaction to needy musicians. This list is simply titled "Things We Say." It consists of short one-liners, used to shut down a conversation or help a player reflect on what they are about to say or do!

As they spoke to me, I took notes!
Things We Say:

- Respond with silence.
- Listen to understand, not to reply.
- Don't apologize.
- "I hear your frustration."
- "In a perfect world…"
- "In your contract it says…"
- "You are part of a collective…"
- "That's interesting."
- "Would you put that in writing?"
- "Unless the rules change, there is nothing I can do."
- "Have you shared that with the orchestra committee?"
- "I'll look into that."
- "Thank you for sharing that."
- "Let's figure out a solution at this level, rather than taking it to the next level," (with Union, Committee, etc.).
- "I didn't hear that, you may want to check with the person who told you."

- "Could I share some information with you?"
- "I think what you are telling me is…"
- "Can I get back to you?"

I've committed all of these statements to memory, to utilize at just the right moment in time.

Journal entry: July 27, 2013, 9:48 a.m.

While sitting in Terminal A, Gate 10 waiting to board flight 7741 to Montreal, I fell witness to the excitement of young travelers. Bursting with energy, parents do their best to control the infectious, uncontainable enthusiasm front of them.

To the contrary, older travelers sit quietly, reading a book or magazine, maybe reviewing their itinerary.

For me, this was a connecting flight which would ultimately end in Edmonton, Canada. Unlike most, but I am sure like some, I had just the proper amount of excitement, anxiety and a twinge of pre-flight jitters.

While waiting on the plane to take off, I made my final preflight phone call home, ending with the proverbial but most sincere "I love you," and "I will call you when we land." The flight attendants are now going through their monolog of safety procedures. My favorite announcement always comes from the cockpit, when they announce "Estimated flight time…" along with the "We will be cruising at …"

As we wheel down the runway, the revolutions of the engine became louder as our speed increases, and soon, we are airborne. As the tires leave the tarmac, I could feel the all familiar gulp, the tensing of my hands as they grip the armrests tighter and tighter. Under our feet, I could feel the landing gear retract to the resting position, where they would spend the next 47 minutes or so locked underneath the aircraft.

I didn't begin to settle down until we were at 32,000 feet. Learning to calm down is something I have wrestled with for years. No matter how much

I have traveled, I still struggle with the process. Perhaps one day, I will overcome, the feeling and be able to enjoy every moment of the experience.

Heading north 590 kilometers, Montreal would be the only stopover on my way to Edmonton. The last time I was in Montreal, I drove the remaining five-and-a-half hours on my own. I was happy to have that memory come flooding back to me while knowing all the while that we had less than an hour until the journey was complete.

The best part of a short flight is that by the time you reach peak altitude and the 'fasten your seatbelt," sign is no longer illuminated, we are instructed to return to our seats and buckle up to prepare for landing.

As the ground comes into view, I could just about read the billboards placed around Pierre Elliott Trudeau International Airport. As the faces in the passing automobiles became recognizable, the wheels of the aircraft touched down. A great rush of air was heard outside as the air brakes began to kick into high gear. We taxied slowly towards the gate, and soon came to a complete stop.

As long as I have been traveling, I will never, ever understand people who immediately leap out of their seats the moment the 'fasten your seatbelt,' signs are turned off. People pop up from their seats, only to have to hold their head sideways to avoid hitting them on the overhead storage area above. I'll pass on the neck ache and remain seated until the departure line reaches my row.

Once in the terminal, there is usually a mile-and-a-half walk to the customs line. No disappointment here, the walk seemed interminable. It is times like this that my daily elliptical workout pays off.

I soon learned there was a one-and-a-half-hour delay in my connecting flight from Montreal to Edmonton. So, I decided to treat myself to a nice sit-down, non-rushed, nutritious meal of tomato soup and a chicken Caesar salad. 26 Canadian dollars later, I headed back to Gate 11.

Before taking off, I was asked by one of the stewardesses' if I wouldn't mind changing my seat to accommodate a couple who were separated, but wished to travel together, I happily obliged. When traveling, no matter how near or far, my preference is always to sit with my wife, so I understood their desire to sit together during the flight.

I must admit that my decision was influenced by the fact I am sure that the passenger who I would be leaving I'm fairly confident hadn't bathed for a week.

Taking off, I followed my predictable behavior of digging my hands into the armrest until the aircraft reaches peak altitude five to seven minutes after takeoff. This time, I cannot recall letting my grip loosen from the armrest for a much longer time than any time in the past. Flight 1179 was incredibly bumpy, all three hours and fifty-seven minutes of it.

Air travel has improved over the years; there is much more we can do to help occupy our time during the flight. In-house movies are playing on the back of the seat in front of you. Television shows games, music, all sorts of entertainment are at your fingertips. I scanned the "Classic Movie" section selected the 1975 blockbuster, JAWS. As I waited for that line in the movie, I made the mistake of relaxing my grip! The plane hit another air pocket and BAM, we dropped what felt like a thousand feet. I pulled my seatbelt tighter around my waist, almost too tight, as I began to gasp for air. Nothing more to do but wait to land, and say a few extra, bargaining prayers to my maker.

Once landed, and after kissing the ground, I headed out to look for the Sky Shuttle for which I had a pre-purchased a transportation ticket, which was $18 Canadian for the advertised 45-minute ride to the hotel. Since leaving home, it has been seven and a half hours plus the 2-hour time change, a hair-raising second flight, and a 45-minute shuttle to my final destination. I was beat.

The advertised time of 45-minutes turned into an hour and twenty minutes. When the shuttle finally dropped me off, I vowed that I would not pay the $18 to return. Instead, I would pay the $55 for a private taxi that would take me directly to the airport. Money well spent!

After checking in at the Westin Hotel on 100th Street, I headed to the restaurant area and ordered a vegetarian flatbread complete, with tomato sauce, Kalamata olives, roasted red pepper, onion, mushroom, tossed arugula, shaved pecorino and "Happy Days Farm," goat cheese along with a side of caramelized brussels sprouts double smoked in bacon lardon. Before receiving the delicious meal, I placed the all-important order of a bottle of Mourvèdre, a full-bodied and rustic wine that I had enjoyed in Spain the summer before.

Content with a most gratifying meal and gratified pallet, I paid the bill and retired to my room for the evening.

Journal entry: July 29, 2014, 1:56 a.m.
The 72-hour conference always leaves me completely energized and revitalized. From the smallest orchestra to the largest, we all face the same issues, problems, and concerns. 7:15 a.m. I am sitting in the hotel café; my overnight bag packed, my printed boarding pass in the left-hand breast pocket of my shirt. Thrilled to have made this journey, gained the knowledge, and enjoyed the company immensely.

Here in the café, the empty chairs slowly begin to fill in with hungry travelers. Some were enjoying their holidays, while others were preparing for meetings. They were all so easy to spot, those with open laptops and half folded newspapers were plainly in the majority, all seemingly preparing for work. Occasionally, you would see someone flag down a waiter to ask for a much-needed refill of coffee.

We are all out of towners, but the workers seemed to be caught up in their personal preparations.

Waiters and waitresses, cooks and busboys are moving all about, in rapid motion – placing checks face down on the tables, cleaning off plates and silverware, replacing the dirty tablecloth with a clean one, for the next hungry group of patrons.

I will be heading back to the airport with my colleague from St. Louis, sharing a cab, as promised, not taking the shuttle.

Back in Edmonton airport, I am waiting to board Air Canada flight 172. From the size of the waiting group, I believe we will have a small aircraft. This brings me to yet another travel pet-peeve I have experienced time after time: passengers stowing their carry-on luggage. The panic looks on their faces, and the anxiousness of the body language, says it all. "What if the compartment above my seat is not available, then what, because I am NOT checking this bag!" As long as I have been traveling, I have needed very little with me, while flying My journal, pencil, eraser, earbuds or earplugs, and some music are all I need.

I watched Jurassic Park with one eye, and with my other, the screen directly in front of the passenger to my right, as he was watching the map. Over Thunder Bay on the shore of Lake Superior, (an impressive sight) passing Ontario just to our north and St. Marie to out south. Further east, we would be flying just north of Lake Huron and south of Georgian Bay. This trip marks the first time I have ever flown over the Great Lakes!

Flight 1478 from Toronto, to Newark, will be the last time I hear the beautiful French language on a flight for a while. Next week, we fly to Zurich, and I imagine it will be Swiss and Italian circling our eardrums as we depart for our well-planned trip to Switzerland, Italy, Croatia, Slovenia, Austria, Germany, and the Czech Republic. I am very much looking forward to this trip and plan to keep a detailed travel log for the duration.

I am feeling complete as a manager with the knowledge that there is more to learn. I believe, more importantly, I feel an understanding of humanity and the needs of those I am working with directly.

These feelings and experiences are the very bits of nourishment needed to keep me engaged and propel me forward. Thank you, Edmonton, for allowing me to experience, understand and grow as a person.

Onward and Upward

"We are rarely proud when we are alone." ~Voltaire

Day after day, I feel blessed to know that I may have made some impact on people's understanding of the amount of concentrated dedication it takes to succeed in the arts.

This particular reviewer of my first book had incredible insight to share. You will see that their three "D's" are different from that of an orchestra personnel manager, yet equally valid in content.

Their comments read in part:
"The general public thinks the world of a professional musician is one of glamor and continuous excitement. Though both are certainly a part of that world, there are countless hours spent in preparation for the exhilarating, most visible moments on stage in front of an audience. Jim Neglia has written a book that describes in detail both the glamour of the work, as well as the daily grind. This very personal account reads as if one is spending the weekend with Jim, listening to his engaging stories, and savoring the descriptions of the food and scenery along the way.

He has written the sort of book many of us say we should someday write, filled with the experiences we have lived and grown through, the trials we've faced, as well as the fun. His work also expresses his indebtedness to those who have taught, supported, and befriended him throughout his career.

For those who are curious about what it's like to be in this particular profession, the writing provides an inside look at the life of a versatile musician. For the reader who is a colleague, the shared realities may yield some absorbing reading.

Neglia puts into words exactly the kind of passion and desire to excel that drives musicians to climb the ladder. It takes courage to put one's heartfelt thoughts from pen to paper for the world to see, but the book is filled with warmth and gratitude, a reminder to all what is most important in life."

Another shared their views on my book, titling their article: "A Beautiful Story About Following Your Passion."

"A guest post from my friend and colleague Jim Neglia, who recently published the book "Onward and Upward," has a truly inspirational story about the relentless determination it takes to succeed in the arts.

The book is an accurate account of his pursuit of a dream career in music. In this around-the-world journey, he shares his stories of culture, family, laughter, friendship, wisdom, and heartache, with a generous splash of the likes of Strauss, motorcycle chases, and Hollywood. Any aspiring artist, would-be world traveler, or entrepreneur, will benefit from reading this book.

> "There is only one success - to be able to spend your
> life in your own way." ~Christopher Morley

For as long as I can remember, I've wanted to be a professional musician. I began my quest hoping beyond hope that my desire alone would be enough to magically propel me to stardom. I soon learned that there are no shortcuts to success, no magic wands to wave; and that my desire was just the tip of the iceberg of what was actually needed to succeed.

Therefore, I changed my approach. I began to settle into a groove that took me on a journey of unparalleled proportions. The journey started by spending countless hours in an eight-foot by eight-foot practice room, determined to sharpen my skills as a budding percussionist. The beginning years were extremely crucial: it was either sink or swim. It was imperative that my dedication takes root and ultimately evolve into my desired profession.

All the hard work, sweat, tears, anxiety, passion, and love ultimately paid off. Years later, I found myself performing with wonderful orchestras and chamber groups, both in the United States and throughout Europe. I had realized an unimaginable goal.

Learning Curve

Many years later, I focused my energy on the next stages of my career: contracting. I saw firsthand, from the perspective of the musician, what it takes to be a successful contractor. Focusing on productions, presentations, preparations, and details seemed a logical starting place. It was during my early performance days that I found myself fascinated by seeing how productions unfolded before my eyes. I thought to myself; Someone had to hire the musicians, work with the union, prepare payroll, and be accountable for the day's events. The more I learned, the more I wanted that person to be me. It was during this transition period from musician to producer that I began keeping detailed notes on how I could best succeed. I also took notes on many other topics, some of which I have included in the pages to come. All the while, keeping my performance chops up to snuff.

Keeping a Journal

More time passed, and I found myself sifting through endless pages of notes, stories, and thoughts I had jotted down over the years. There were such a variety of offerings and I knew I needed to begin organizing my thoughts more carefully. In doing so, I was able to choose some of the more ridiculous, interesting, absurd, but hopefully, entertaining anecdotes to share with you.

Accountability Partners

There were many people responsible for nurturing, and pushing me to offer these stories. They knew exactly when their support was needed the most. These are the same people who, years before, had pushed me to work harder on the music I was preparing, who picked me up from the practice room floor when I had fallen asleep from exhaustion, who helped push me beyond the limits of the normal, and they showed me how to achieve the impossible. These are the people who have helped make my life as successful as it could be. I wish to thank them all. I think of my dear friend Ray, mentor Chuck, Brother Joe, wife Alexandra, and others who helped show me that hard work and determination were indeed a good thing. Be relentless in your passion, steadfast in your drive, and you will achieve all that is possible.

The 3 "D's."

In the pursuit of any career, one needs the proper guidance and support. This idea, along with the ability to recognize the help offered to succeed, were constant thoughts in my mind. I was taught about the three Ds, all of which have served as daily reminders to stay on the road of my chosen path: drive, determination, and devotion have all served me well. I have kept these principles in the forefront of my being all these years. I was fortunate during the early days to recognize these essential elements, and with each step, albeit baby ones, I slowly traveled feet, yards, and, miles.

Cannobio

"I can speak to my soul only when the two of us are off exploring deserts or cities or mountains or roads." ~Paulo Coelho

August 12, Day 5, 40 Kilometers

Always go with your instincts, that is my advice. On the day we landed from the United States and made our journey to Stresa, we passed through a small town, Cannobio. As we crossed the city limits and entered the town, we were taken back by its soothing atmosphere. People could be seen milling about, enjoying a slow stroll, or sharing conversation over a cup of coffee in the open-air cafes. There were tents set up along the cobblestone road, up and down the city street in a festive setting. I wanted to stop immediately, but feared the effects that travel would have on me before long. Instead, I made a mental note of the town and thought it might be a beautiful place to visit at some point during the next few days and came back a few days later to do just that.

We approached the city for the second time on our trip but this time from the south via Carmine. Just 3 kilometers away, we followed the SS34 which was hugging the endless beauty of Lake Maggiore. I kept my eye out for the small blue parking signs.

Once parked, we made our way to the far side of the parking lot where a passageway was waiting for us. This opening placed us at the top of a steep cobblestone stairwell. At the bottom of the stairs, hidden from the roadway, was the quaint village-like town of Cannobio which sat on the sublime shoreline of Lago Maggiore.

At the bottom of the steps, we walked under a 13th-century archway and found ourselves staring at the precipice of this adorable, medieval town. As our eyes panned from left to right, we saw a long line of shops opposite the Lake.

There was a wide variety of stores, that offered everything from clothing to pastry, from brick-o-brack, to cosmetics. Sitting on a wooden cutting board just north of the doorway was a pile of salami samples! Covering the façade of the buildings were hanging meats, which were white-powdered and delicious to the eye. I am not a big meat eater, but I believe we sampled more than eight in total, each with a different texture and taste, all bursting with flavor.

Continuing past the salami shop, we stumbled on a supermarket where we made purchases to compliment the waiting salami feast: crusty bread, a block of cheese, a container of cherry tomatoes, a bottle of mineral water with gas, and the most delicious container of soft jumbo shrimp in an oil and herb base.

After paying the cashier, we headed back towards the salami shop to find a spot in the shade to begin our feast. Just in front of the store was a concrete and brick wall. Cut into the wall were double seats placed strategically every few meters. We found a perfect spot, in the shade with a beautifully built-in-seat just adjacent to our chosen area.

We unwrapped each parcel and began to spread out the food along the brick wall. There we were, enjoying some of the most gratifying, mouthwatering eatables with a view overlooking the grandiose Lake Maggiore. On the Lake, moving all about were sailboats as well as feet-propelled and motorboats alike. Much like visiting a large museum, one can only take in so much in any given visit. That is where I was now; I couldn't soak in anymore. I was utterly saturated with our surroundings and felt at one with Cannobio.

When I experience such a transformation is when I realize the total happiness in a particular area. I feel a sense of complete contentment.

Back in Stresa, I ventured out of our comfortable hotel. Just a few blocks away was a charming establishment, Caffe Bolongaro, where we could sit down, enjoy a nice bottle of wine, and begin to relive the events of the day. I did so while uploading a good number of photographs from my trusty Wi-Fi-enabled camera to Facebook. I took complete advantage of my new surroundings and a never-ending glass of wine. I remained seated and wrote in my journal for several hours, breaking my rule for writing my recap the morning after.

As I wrote, my pencil kept sliding from my greasy fingers, remnants of the salami long since gone.

Tomorrow, Milano.

Johnny Mathis

Chances Are

It was in the spring of 1999 when I received a phone call to book the musicians for the incomparable, Johnny Mathis. After learning the dates and times of the services, I asked the all-important question: can you let me know the exact instrumentation needed? The answer came in shortly from the music director of Johnny Mathis himself: 27 musicians in total.

Mathis travels with his music director, who doubles as his pianist, guitarist/manager as well as his bassist and drum set player.

My next task was to create the budget and present it to the venue. Included in the proposal were all the needed required costs, those being rehearsal and performance salaries, pension and health benefit obligations as well as all rental and cartage for the harpist and percussionist. Additionally, I calculated the work dues deductions so my numbers would be precise.

Once all numbers are in place, I submit the completed budget and wait for approval. Once I receive approval along with the timing of each service, I can begin securing the musicians.

Before doing any hiring, I received an email from the music director, requesting a list of players he would like me to secure. I love it when a music director has specific players they want me to secure, as it serves me well. By hiring those players, it protects me from any scrutiny of a lousy performance by a given musician. After all, I hired who I was told to hire.

In this case, the Music Director was spot on, nearly all of the players he requested were already in my trusty personnel file, all marvelous musicians, and all wonderful people. There were only a few I did not know so well, one of which was the percussionist.

Once I begin my work, the personnel started falling into place with relative ease. When I called the percussionist, Ed, we chatted about the specifics of the gig. When we discussed the list, he informed me that he would prefer to bring many of the smaller, handheld instruments for the date. I agreed. I recall asking him when he started playing with Johnny— "Since 1969." Enough said.

Once the final player was secured, there was nothing left to do but wait for the day to come. I remember the night before, lying in bed struggling to fall asleep. Two things kept going through my mind over and over. The first, was that I was incredibly fortunate to be doing what I enjoy doing with my life. I get to, employ musicians and be immersed in the thick of it, playing my part in the positive process of the entertainment industry.

The second, was equally earth-shattering to me, I was about to meet a legend in the entertainment world. I mean, this was Johnny Mathis! He began his professional career in 1956, seven years before I was born, and he is still going strong. This thought alone was staggering to me. He is the artist who recorded such great tunes as "It's Not For Me To Say," "Misty," "Wonderful! Wonderful!" and the smash hit "Chances Are." I was excited beyond words to be part of what was about to happen.

The day of the gig I dragged myself out of bed, a bit bleary-eyed. Although I was exhausted from the short night sleep, I was invigorated with the excitement of what awaited me that day.

Once I parked and entered the hall, I checked in with the venue manager to let them know I had arrived. After checking in, I headed to the stage to see the configuration and placement of the chairs. The strings were set up all on stage right, and the brass, saxophones, and trumpets were on stage left. Center stage, closest to the audience was the piano, and just to the left of the piano were the guitar, electric bass, and drum set. Finally, two four by 8-foot platforms held what was the enormous percussion setup.

As I continued to scan the stage, my eyes kept coming back to the percussion section, or should I say, the percussion solo player, Mr. Ed. As I glanced at it for the third time, Ed appeared from underneath it, hunched over, tightening a cymbal and trap table stands. It seemed like an opportune time to go and meet the percussionist before the show.

"Hey, you must be Jim; it's nice to meet you," Ed told me as I approached. That statement was my introduction to a person who was soon to become a lifelong friend.

Ed was a warm, sensitive, and conscientious type. He arrived nearly two hours early, which demonstrated his integrity as a player. Working with so many musicians, management personnel, producers, and publicists over the years, I have learned how to read people and their intentions rather quickly.

I panned Ed's set up from left to right, paying close attention to all the smaller handheld instruments he supplied. The thing that caught my eye was the unbelievable assortment of shakers he had prepared. He had shakers from the smallest egg to the large torpedo style, placed strategically on his trap table. I didn't want to take further time away from his set up, so I politely excused myself.

Just after 2 p.m., the music director walked onto the stage. "Is that you Jim?" he uttered, and just like that, our relationship was born. I informed him of the required break times for the musicians and that I would be back a few minutes before 2:30 to get started.

By 2:15, the majority of the musicians came to the stage to take a peek at the charts that were being performed. At 2:25, I took hold of the stage phone and. I announced, "Places please, 4 minutes to tuning". At precisely 2:30, the rehearsal began.

One by one, the Music Director would call our charts, "Okay, take a look at "Too Much Too Late Too Little," this is how it works."

He would explain parts that were repeated, how many times, and if there was a vamp, what his signal would be to get us out of the vamp. The Music Director was the real deal, a true professional who had mastered the art of the rehearsal. Sitting on the sideline observing, I noticed that 40 minutes had passed and Johnny Mathis still hadn't arrived. Drawing on past experience, I recalled that most headliners work this way, showing up at the end of the rehearsal to touch on just a few numbers.

Without notice, appearing on stage left was, Mr. Johnny Mathis. I nearly fell off my chair, seeing him. The Music Director stopped what he was doing and introduced Mr. Mathis to the musicians. There was a warm shuffle from the group before continuing as if nothing had happened. All became abundantly clear in the minutes to come; Johnny performed many works without the full ensemble, which is why the group had run nearly all the charts before his arrival.

During a lecture I gave at the New York chapter of the Percussive Arts Society, a participant asked me if there had ever been a time where I felt I was being tested as a contractor? I recalled my Johnny Mathis test quite well.

The next tune was called specifically by Johnny himself; "Let's Run Brazil." A 1, 2, a 1, 2, 3, 4 and they were off.

Brazil is a Latin-based tune which has a strong rhythm section accompaniment, all of which is led by the percussionist. About 10 or 12 measures into the selection, Mathis stopped the band, "I can't hear the shakers, Ed, do you have any bigger shakers?" he asked. Ed tossed down the egg size shakers and upgraded to next size up.

Mathis counts off again, 1, 2, a 1, 2, 3, 4 and off they went. This time the ensemble only performed about eight measures before Mathis cut off the tune stating he still couldn't hear the shakers.

I began to panic since this was *my* player up there. Yes, I know, I got his name from the music director, but still, anyone on the stage is ultimately my responsibility. I can honestly tell you; I was feeling responsible for the lack of judgment on the part of Ed and his shaker selections.

Once again, Mathis directed his attention towards Ed and asked for a more substantial sound, something that would cut through the volume. Ed nodded his head once again and replaced the soft sounding shakers with something he felt was more suitable. Mathis shouts out, 1, 2, a 1, 2, 3, 4! This time I am nervous for Ed AND myself, as I was beginning to think this was the first and last time I would work with the considerable talent before my eyes.

I listened carefully, and sure enough, these shakers were loud, I mean, really loud. I would never have chosen such a set for this work or any work for that matter as I felt they were too loud. Mathis stopped the orchestra and began to sound speak and he sounded very unhappy, this being the third time he stopped the orchestra on the same tune, before even singing a note. I begin to think up excuses for why Ed was having such difficulties, since I felt the need to protect myself. I thought Ed was a solid player, with great timing, so was perplexed as to why he was screwing this up so royally? Just like that, all of my incredible wisdom on "sizing up a person," went out the window.

Mathis called off 1-2, a 1-2-3-4 and the band began to play, but this time, there were no shakers at all! I could feel my blood rushing to my face! I was beside myself with disappointment and was searching for some excuse I could offer Mathis for the lack of professionalism from Ed. I nearly soiled my pants!

As I was thinking about what to say, my internal clock was ticking to the music and felt that at least 24 measures had passed. 24 measures, 24 measures, this is almost four times more than before, but how can it be?

At that moment, I looked over at Ed and saw that he had knelt down behind the vibraphone and had begun to pull out a wide cylindrical PVC pipe filled with beads. He was laying down a rhythm like you never heard before. Ed performed precisely!

My mind and eyes were racing and scanning the information, noticing that Mathis himself was smiling, then laughing, then *really* laughing as was the Music Director. What? I was in need of an underwear change, and they were all laughing?!

As I moved towards Ed who was holding up a gigantic homemade, loud, rugged shaker in his hands, I couldn't help but notice the writing across the front of the instrument itself. As I twisted my neck around to see the inscription, everyone on the stage was laughing. All of the musicians, the music director, Johnny, and above all Ed, all seemingly laughing at me. There it was, in full view of everyone else until that moment, the inscription on the shaker itself read: "The Johnny Mathis shaker for the hearing impaired." At that moment, all of my fears turned to laughter, along with the rest of my colleagues. I didn't even need to change my pants! It was at that moment I realized that the entire ensemble, music director, Mathis himself, and of course Ed, were all in on the initiation joke. It seemed that this was their way of accepting me into the Mathis family. It was at that moment that I knew it was best that I never, ever, take my work SO seriously.

In between the rehearsal and performance, I had a chance to speak with Ed. We chatted about his vast experience as a percussionist, as well as his ability to keep a great poker face on! I loved his honesty and genuine spirit. I immediately knew my initial summation of Ed was correct.

When I recognized him as "Shakers," or better yet, Ed "Shakers" Shea, I baptized him for all of eternity, as nickname "Shakers" has stuck with him to this day. For at least the past 15 years, Shakers and I have enjoyed a true friendship.

Milan

"The impulse to travel is one of the hopeful symptoms of life."
~Agnes Repplier

August 13, Day 6, 95 Kilometers

Pulling off the A8, we veered onto Viale Alcide De Gasperi, then left onto Viale Renato Serra, and right again onto Corso Sempione. Following Sempione through a zigzag of mazes, we finally came upon what looked like the center.

Driving through the streets became more challenging. I was unsure exactly where to place the car, as there were no real defined car lanes and we shared the same part of the roadway with the electric tram lanes. When turning onto Corso Sempione, I found myself driving on the tram track with no possibility of getting back on the main road. I had to jump the tracks to get back on the roadway designated for vehicles other than trams. What a mess.

I needed to park our car before I found myself driving on a more dangerous part of the roadway. I asked the passengers o to be on the lookout for a garage.

After hearing, "there," from the back seat, I pulled to the right into an open parking spot. I got out to read the parking signs to make sure the spot was legal, recalling the parking tickets I had received in Aosta, Italy, and Pisa some years earlier.

A man was standing in front of the building where I was considering parking our car. Before turning the engine off, I got out and approached him. "Do you speak Italian?" At which he said, "Sì, ma tu sono ovviamente americani, per favore parlano Inglese," which translates to "Yes but you are clearly American, so please speak English." A tad disappointed, I quickly switched to English.

He informed me that the parking spot that our car was parked in was for diplomatic clients only. He directed us to a municipal lot just a block away. After thanking the man, I followed his directions. As we entered the garage, we drove down two levels to find a vacant parking spot. The parking spots were all small, so small I couldn't imagine how I was going to squeeze our larger rental car into an empty place.

Slowly and with determination, I shimmied in and out of a narrow spot in the nearby garage, until I landed our car between the designated white lines. When we emerged from the underground parking area, all of the harsh memories I had of Milan vanished instantly; permanently erased from my mind. The city has remarkable character and charm. I usually shy away from the larger cities of Europe (with the exception of Paris, Rome, and Barcelona) because I prefer smaller, more intimate cities and villages. Although Milan is the second most populous city in Italy after Rome, I found Milan was a cross between the little villages and the large cities. I was enjoying the vibe of our new surroundings.

I asked the attendant "Come posso arrivare al Teatro alla Scala? (How do I get to La Scala)?" "When you come outside of the garage, travel in the opposite direction of the entrance. At the end of the road, make a left past the Galleria Vittorio Emanuele II. Teatro La Scala will appear just past Il Duomo," he responded.

Following his directions, we soon saw Il Duomo in the near distance. The structure was grandiose in size and Gothic in style, towering over all of the downtown area.

Saint Ambrose's New Basilica was built on this site at the beginning of the 5th century, with an adjoining basilica added a few hundred years later. The old Baptistry, Battistero Paleocristiano, can still be visited under the Milan Cathedral and is one of the oldest Christian buildings in all of Europe.

Just to the right of Corso Vittorio was Via Tommaso. A short 120 meters later, we came across Piazza Della Scala, and ultimately, Via Filodrammatici.

There it was, directly in front of us, the famed Teatro alla Scala. Another stunning sight during our travels came into focus. We were excited by the sheer anticipation of our visit which was yet to come.

It was impossible to not ponder all of the incredible talent which has performed in this great hall. Artists such as Pavarotti, Abbado, Toscanini, Callas, Di Stefano, and Gigli have played in the building we were about to enter ourselves. Wanting to explore the inside of the theater, we purchased our tickets to have a look for ourselves.

We climbed the two flights of steps to the entrance of the main theater. Covering every inch of the two-flight staircase along the wall, were billboards of concerts and operas from the past. Opera after opera, billboard after billboard, commemorating a passage in time. La Traviata, Othello, Don Giovanni, The Marriage of Figaro, Carmen, The Magic Flute, Don Juan, Electra and dozens more were all represented. I felt the electricity in the air, the music all around us, the joy awaiting us. I was alive with excitement.

Upon entering the grand foyer, one couldn't miss the stunning statue of La Scala's favorite sons. The décor of the room is unassuming, yet overwhelming. Adorned with hardwood floors, red velvet curtains, Greek-style pillars, ornate crown molding, three stunning crystal chandeliers and busts of Toscanini, Mascagni, Puccini, and Wagner. A sight to behold.

Directly behind Toscanini's bust, was one of the many entrances into the hall. In the viewing box, we found ourselves looking directly at the stage from the center of the audience, from the second tier. Plush velvet covered the hall, dark maroon-reddish upholstery everywhere; it was an impressive sight.

The orchestra pit was enormous, affording plenty of elbow room for the cello, bass and percussion sections. What took place both on and below the stage, the depth of talent, poise, promise, and general musicianship, didn't go unnoticed. Even in the emptiness of the hall, the depths of its history was there before our eyes, below our feet and deep, within our hearts.

I could imagine watching a presentation of an opera in such a lavish hall, with its superb design. I also imagined what it would be like to perform in this magnificent space. Lost in thought, Sasha asked me nearly simultaneously if I could imagine what it would be like playing in that pit! I just chuckled and welcomed her to my imagination.

In the grand foyer, we entered the museum itself. As we entered the room, the first thing we saw was an impressive selection of musical instruments: a virginal painted by Guaracino in 1667, a few psalteries, lutes and lyre-guitars, the Sommer fortepiano that belonged to Giuseppe Verdi.

Around the instruments, was a 17th Century painting by Baschenis, just below it is a showcase of more antique instruments. There was a bust of Verdi, sculpted by Gemito, and below that, as a historical thread linking the two La Scala protagonists, a portrait of Piermarini, the architect who was called by Empress Maria Theresa to build the Teatro alla Scala. We saw a Baschenis oil painting called Strumenti Musicali, a still life of musical instruments placed with elegance on a table covered with an Oriental carpet. Ceramics of every sort, busts, oil paintings, artifacts, and relics owned by every opera star who performed in the grand theater. Items once owned by Giuseppe Verdi, Franz Liszt, Arturo Toscanini, Giacomo Puccini, and more. I could spend an hour peering into just one of the dozens of showcases filled with memories of those illustrious performers who worked at La Scala.

Seeing Verdi's piano was difficult to digest, it was hard to believe he played and composed music on the very instrument that sits before my eyes. Additionally, Franz Liszt's piano was also in the museum, which boasted that the instrument was still in use today, yes in the 21st century. My heart began to fill up with emotion, as my eyes began to well up with tears.

These are the composers whose music I have studied and performed may have been conceived on these very instruments. All the factors came together as I became overwhelmed with the mystery of music, my chosen field, and source of love.

As if this experience wasn't enough, the highlights were yet to come. I entered the back room and was moved to such heights, such exhilaration I could no longer hold back my emotion.

Scanning the items under the glass, the glittering of a gold pocket watch caught my eye. There was a tiny, but still legible, label which read, "Puccini." As someone who has studied Puccini's signature for years, knew what I was viewing. I was stunned, nearly in shock, at the watch.

The second item which took my breath away was a conductor's baton. It was the very baton used by Arturo Toscanini, during his final performance at La Scala. I considered how much music that baton made, which boggled my mind to process.

I later learned, that after sixty plus years association with the orchestra at La Scala, dating back to 1887, Toscanini gave his final concert recital with the orchestra on September 19, 1952, with an ecstatically received, all Wagner program.

The performance ran nearly two full hours and consisted of Die Meistersinger, Siegfried: Forest Murmurs, Siegfried Idyll, and Götterdämmerung: Siegfried's Rhine Journey. After the interval, the program continued with Parsifal: Good Friday Spell, Götterdämmerung: Siegfried's Death & Funeral Music, Tristan und Isolde: Prelude and Liebestod and concluding with Die Valkyries, The Ride of the Valkyries. An enormous send off to the father of La Scala.

The final item, the crème de la crème was housed under glass and for good reason. Below the sparkling glass was an open score to one of my favorite works in the entire classical music repertoire. A thick handwritten score, written entirely in the hand of Giuseppe Verdi. The score was of his grand mass of death, his Requiem. If you couldn't read music, there was no way of knowing what you were looking at, as the score was open to page 50. As I looked down at the score, I read the moving lines of the violins, in rapid 16th notes sounding out the passage of the almighty Dies Irae.

I was enthralled, not only because of the greatness of the music set before me, but that this music was one of a kind.

I stood in amazement for what felt like an hour. I pulled out my camera, so I could take a snapshot of this fantastic score. Just before clicking the memory, I notice a sign that read "NO Pictures." I respected the notice and obeyed. To this day, I have the score captured in my private picture viewer.

Not able to digest one item more, we knew it was time to take our leave.

On our drive back from Milan to Stresa, I could not get the score out of my mind. In my mind, I reached for the "on," button on the radio and tuned to the Requiem. The requiem was now playing. With each measure that sang in my head, it seemed another kilometer passed. Before I knew it, we were back in Stresa in the comforts of our lavish hotel.

Still humming, I packed our bags and prepared for our trip to Venice in the morning.

Discovery

"The study of the past is the main portal through
which culture is acquired." ~Joseph Epstein

In preparation for my mother selling her house, I helped clear out her rarely
seen belongings, which were tucked away in the attic.

We used an old lighting system to see what was in the far reaches of the
area under the eaves of the house, that being an Edison light bulb on a pull
string. We had always relied on the trusty Edison to illuminate the dimly
lit area and, under normal conditions, it worked. On this particular day,
the weather forecast called for showers, so it was dark and dreary outside.
As a result, the Edison wasn't enough to light up the area I need to clear.

I grabbed a small lamp and plugged it into the waiting outlet. Now, I was
able to get to work. I wasn't sure what I was looking for or if I was even
looking for anything at all. My focus shifted through what we should keep
and what we could add to a future garage sale.

After sorting through endless boxes, I spotted a large trunk tucked into
the far reaches of the attic. Moving closer, I was so severely crowded by the
eaves, I had to hunch over.

Stretching my right arm as far as I could reach, I was able to get my hand on the leather strap handle. Tightening my grip, I began tugging at the trunk. Realizing that the weight of the truck was too much for just one hand and the weakened leather strap, I instead resorted to crouching over on all fours. From that position, I was able to get my hands on the top of the chest. Sliding the chest one inch at a time, I eventually was able to get a better grip and move it away from where it had lived for the past 30 years.

Once out from under the constraints of the eaves, I pulled the trunk toward me and into the adjacent room to have a look at its contents.

Upon first glance, I see a monogram on the center of the lid. The initials revealed a simple E.W. I later learned that the trunk came with the house and the E.W. represented the initials of the previous owner, Ellen Wilson. My parents must have used the trunk as a storage piece when they moved into the house back in May of 1969.

As I opened the lid and took my first look, all I could see were papers. I saw stacks of paper, not just any paper but stack after stack of manuscript papers! To add to my already treasured find, I soon became aware that the manuscript paper was in the original hand of whoever composed the music.

My heart skipped a beat in anticipation of learning who penned the manuscripts. I picked up the first batch of papers and focused on the upper right-hand corner to see the name of the composer. It was none other than my great uncle, Francesco Paolo Neglia.

In the trunk, I discovered so many of my great uncle's treasures. There were many musical selections, complete scores of his works, individual parts for complete symphonies, solo works, piano, and the mandolin selections. There were full scores and individual instrumental parts to his string quartets, piano trios, and opera extracts. All of these scores were seeing the light for the first time since being placed in the attic back in 1969.

Finding the musical selections sent me a reminder of what I have always known: I am Francesco's direct descendant and a musician who is holding an incredible amount of his music and family history in my hands and heart.

Due to my early separation from my father in 1976, when I was 13, I had no connection to our family genealogy. With the discovery of this treasure trove of music offerings, I became curious to learn more about my great uncle.

"The seeker embarks on a journey to find what he wants and discovers, along the way, what he needs." ~Wally Lamb

I was mildly interested in collecting autograph material because I had been meeting many personalities in the music field while at work. Each time I would work with a person of notoriety, I would ask them to sign a photograph, my actual sheet music, or write me a short note.

While walking the streets of Vienna in 1995, I stumbled onto an Autograph Shoppe. The establishment was tucked away on one of the less busy Vienna streets; Dorotheergasse. Here, my short visit to Palais Dorotheum only intensified my interest in autograph collecting.

I soon learned that Palais Dorotheum was celebrating 300 plus years since its foundation in Vienna by Emperor Joseph I in 1707. Dorotheum is the largest auction house in German-speaking Europe, as well as a leader in Central Europe. It is also one of the oldest and largest auction houses in the world.

With my newly acquired knowledge, I asked the proprietor where I could view their current selection of classical composer's autographs. directed me to a series of black binders that were sitting on the center counter. The spine of the first binder read "Composers A-F." Sitting next to that binder was another which read "Composers G-L." I understood the concept and picked up book 1, composers A to F.

As I opened the book, the first thing I saw was listings of composers. Next, to each name, there was an indication of the actual item that are for sale. There were acronyms such as ANS which meant, Autograph Note Signed, ALS, SP or AMusQ representing Autograph Letter Signed, Signed Picture, and Autograph Musical Quote – the quotes were literally hand-written music quotes from selections that the composer chose to include in his signature. Absolutely fascinating!

After the A's came the likes of Bartok and Brahms; my head began to ache. I asked the assistant to bring me the specified catalog number, and a few short moments later, I would be holding in my hands the requested item; an actual letter that Johannes Brahms wrote in 1872. From this day forward, I was under the spell of collecting these treasures for my consumption.

Music is a very broad category to collect, so I knew I needed to narrow my field of collecting to only one, one that truly captivated me and my imagination: composers.

Over the years, I have done my best to keep my interest focused on collecting documents, photographs, and calling cards of classical composers. However, an occasional conductor, soloist or other notable falls on my lap that I feel compelled to add it to my budding collection.

What am I really collecting? Consider an autographed letter, something penned by one of the masters. That letter represents the only document of its kind, an original, as there are no copies. When a written letter refers to a specific topic, such as a visit with another composer, or references a specific composition, travel plans, new commissions, or family matters, the letter becomes more desirable. Signed photographs, especially those that the composer pens a few measures of music become even more valuable.

As my interest grew, I began to understand that there are a lot of untrustworthy people and dealers in the world. In response, I started studying forensic handwriting for signature comparison, a few years after becoming a collector. As the years passed, I have become more adept at telling when a signature is live or a facsimile, an original or a forgery.

I have been collecting autographs and ephemera about composers for the better part of 23 years, and my collection has grown exponentially. At the time of writing, my collection exceeds 600 pieces.

Francesco Paolo Neglia

"Music is a higher revelation than all wisdom and philosophy."
~Ludwig van Beethoven

Via Paolo Vetri, Birthplace of Neglia

IN THIS HOUSE HE WAS BORN
FRANCESCO PAOLO NEGLIA
GLORIOUS MUSICIAN OF ITALY
HE LIVED HERE

REDUCE BY TRUMP IN FOREIGN LAND
MORE YEARS INTENSE OF HIS LIFE
COMFORTING IN PEACE OF ROOMS MEMORI
HIS SPIRIT TRAVAGLIATO
FROM ADVERSITY OF DESTINY

THE CITY OF ENNA
THIRTY YEAR AFTER DEATH
HONORS IN THIS MARBLE
THE GREAT SON INSCRIBED NAME
AMONG THE PIONEERS MORE
OF ITALIAN SYMBOLISM
A PERMANENT RECORD FOR FUTURE GENERATIONS
XXXI. VII. MCMLXII

After spending a tremendous amount of time researching and gathering information on my great uncle's life, all of which are written in Italian, I translated the text to the best of my ability. I am sharing it in this chapter.

Many do not know his name, and yet the activity of this praised conductor, composer, and entrepreneur rival that of his contemporaries.

Francesco Paolo Neglia was a native of Castrogiovanni, now Enna, Sicily. He was born on May 22, 1874, into a musical family. His father Joseph was a violinist and choirmaster at the local cathedral. His mother, Maria was a primary school music teacher.

As a boy, Francesco played the violin in the cathedral chapel orchestra as well as the city theater. By the time he finished his studies at the age of 19, he had become an elementary school teacher in his hometown. A year later, Francesco moved to Palermo, where he studied at the Conservatory with William Zuelli and graduated with high honors in violin performance, conducting and composition. For some time after his graduation, he devoted himself to conducting, overseeing the coordination of operas in several Italian theaters.

On December 17, 1900, at the age of 26, he married Marie Dibbern, whose family was of German origins but lived in Taormina. After many failed attempts to kick-start his career in Sicily, he decided to relocate to Hamburg, Germany.

Once in Germany, he gained nearly immediate notoriety as a musician. So much so, in fact, he established the Akademisches Musik-Institut. Later in 1908, the conservatory was renamed Neglia Konservatorium which boasted an enrollment that exceeded 500 students.

After founding the Conservatory in Germany, his conducting career began to take off. In a brief time, the newspapers would classify him as amongst the most significant interpreters of the Beethoven symphonies in the land. These reviews lead to many invitations for him to conduct the highest orchestras of Berlin, Kiel, Bad-Nauheim, Frankfort on Mein, as well as the famous Stadt Theater in the company of the famed Felix Weingartner.

As a result of his conducting engagements, the public had a clear idea of the spiritual and cultural heights derived from Neglia's abilities. A Sicilian was now rivaling the heights of his now fellow Germans.

A critical review of the Hamburg Fremdenblatt regards Neglia in the following statement:

"The difficulties that are met for the performance of Bruckner's Symphonies may be a justification never to hazard their execution: with an orchestra, which can interpret the nine symphonies of Bruckner as our Musik Freunde Orchestra has interpreted it, everything can be ventured. The execution was an excellent beauty and of the penetrating truth. To have led the orchestra to this perfection is behind discussion merit of Professor Neglia."

Neglia was also known as a great interpreter of both Verdi and Bruckner. There are a multitude of glowing reviews to read during his illustrious career. He shared a great friendship with his contemporaries, among them were Marco Enrico Bossi whose principal symphonic works Neglia made known, most notably his Concerto for organ Op. 100.

Neglia never failed to help his fellow countrymen. As a response to the horrible news he was reading, of, the loyal servant lends his helping hand. On the occasion of the Messina earthquake in 1908, Neglia organized and directed a grand concert which yielded the net proceeds of 25,000 francs. This money was handed out directly to the survivors of the disaster. His name and fame had become famous in all of Germany as well as Italy.

Due to his father's death, (which coincided with the outbreak of World War I), he returned to his home of Sicily but was met with little enthusiasm by his countrymen. In fact, the inhabitants of Enna were suspicious of Francesco, who had lived his life in Germany and brought in tow a wife and three children, all of whom were of German descent.

The dignitaries of the city of Enna stood in Neglia's way. They impeded all efforts to share his talents and musicianship he had learned in a foreign land. The local council even failed to support Francesco to fill the modest post of conductor of the Enna Cathedral.

The outbreak of the war had massive effects on the Neglia's. Francesco's wife could not leave the house, because she was singled out and suspected as being a German spy. Their children were unfortunately targeted and stoned by their peers as they were considered to be foreign spies as well.

In spite of the interest taken in him by Marco Enrico Bossi, Giacomo Puccini, and Richard Strauss, he could find no work as a musician. Soon, Neglia was relegated to the role of an ordinary hack. Even his private mail was confiscated, for fear that subsidies he received by the Austrians may have been for espionage services rendered to the Germans.

However, Neglia did not give up. He was able to find a bit of serenity when he moved to Caltanissetta, where he would conduct the city's orchestra.

His desire to resume a more profound musical career led him to move just northwest of Milan, to the town of Legnano, far from Sicily. There, he took a position as an elementary school teacher and was the first person of his generation to envision the inclusion of music in all schools at all levels. As a result, he founded the School of Music "Verdi."

It was then that he began composing again. About an hour to the east of Legnano in the city of Lombardy, he completed his only opera, "Zelia." He also wrote the final work of his lifetime, his beautiful Piano Trio Opus 52.

The year before his death, he began to suffer from symptoms of nephritis (inflammation of the kidneys), which lead him ultimately to his death on July 31, 1932, where he died on the shore of Lake Maggiore in the waterside city Intra. Years later, the proud people of Legnano named a street after him, Via Francesco Paolo Neglia.

While researching my great Uncle, I came across many more fantastic reviews.

"From Maestro Neglia's production, it detaches the physiognomy neatly onto a musician nourished with very good and rather classical studies, where it does not overhang the impetus of his exuberant temperament, burning with Southern warmth, unaltered by the northern temperatures so favorable to him in the dawn of his artistic career."

For many years, Neglia regularly collaborated with the Stadttheater Hamburg. He would alternate on the podium with Felix Weingartner, one of the most important conductors of the early 20th century. The prestigious position increased his reputation significantly, so much so that in 1910 Biergfeld, critical magazine *Signal für die, Musikalische Welt,* called Neglia "One of the best interpreters," of Beethoven's Nine Symphonies, while the Heinrich Chevalley wrote in the pages of the Hamburger Fremdenblatt:

"I know dozens of German directors, who, as children of the Country, feel the rumble rivulet of Beethoven (Pastoral) where they grew up, to which no one ever opens, as Neglia, the precise image of the event to describe the nature."

In 1912, he returned to direct Beethoven's Ninth and First symphonies, ultimately arousing the full consent of the public and critics:

"Professor Neglia directed both works from memory. That certainly not simple exhibitionism but for the Neglia, which is averse to any form of presentation, it means something else. From this, in fact, you can see not only the necessary

familiarity with the compositions to be performed but also the love, even moving to a foreigner that proves to Neglia's Beethoven. This allows tireless dedication to Neglia's ever deeper understanding of the spiritual world great music creator. This gradual maturation has not done Neglia a musician sophisticated and pedantic, which moves only on crutches of reason, nor will ever become such. He is a musician who has a heart above all. Gave the last time the superlative desired, ethics without spiritual which you cannot have the mood to be the triumphed over all adversity."

Ferdinand Pfohl, German musicologists, wrote in the nella Hamburger Nachrichten (Hamburg news):

"A great deal of satisfaction ... must have procured the eminent director of the fact of being closely followed in his worthy initiative - elected by a cheering crowd. ... And who would deny this success to the loyal, diligent Neglia, exciting artist, exemplary in its idealism."

The same outlet stressed the personality is not typical in a Sicilian composer in 1910:

"That Director fiery and able to dominate with the unquestioned safety of the orchestra, which we have it known and appreciated in its orchestral concerts, always based on a great idealism and a personal joy of sacrifice."

Neglia's qualities emerged and became increasingly evident during the execution of works of music that were more technically more complex. An example of this can be found in *The Symphony of Glory* by Jean-Louis Nicodè. This symphony is an enormous stride in both ambition and scope. The work calls for an augmented orchestra, singers, staging, and a duration of 150 minutes. *The Symphony of Glory* is to Nicodé what *Ein Heldenleben* is to Strauss.

Neglia took on the monumental task and performed the Symphony before the public in Hamburg on October 26, 1908. The following day the Hamburger news so wrote:

"Master Neglia, continuing his work mainly and disinterested for the presentation of new works, included in the program of his first symphony concert of the season. The Symphony of Glory Jean-Louis Nicodè, a colossal amount of work reminiscent of strange architectural constructions that rise and you break down into tiny gardens, medieval ramparts, and battlements.

Neglia has obtained great artistic merit for its initiative and the excellent command of the extraordinarily complicated score. Directing with a temper on and with remarkable foresight, in his way, he remembered very often Max Fiedler, with whom he shared the lively line of gestures, the style exterior and also the joy passionate, their enjoyment in directing. A presence of sympathy leaves the artistic impression of loyalty and selfless abandonment destinations to high art. The outcome of the work was unusually friendly and culminated at the end with an amazing call to the director and composer."

Six years later, Neglia decided to tackle another even more complex work, The Oratorio Quo Vadis, which was composed a few years earlier (in 1907) by the Polish musician Feliks Nowowiejski. The work had not yet been performed in German theaters, due to a massive practical presence. In this case, the composition requires the inclusion of about five hundred performers. Neglia took on the project with the utmost determination and professionalism.

The German newspapers rewarded Neglia's consistent dedication with many publications and reviews clearly, all being positive. The reviews included the March 22 nella Hamburger Fremdenblatt that boasted the spontaneity talent of this *"brave idealist"* who had *"received an implementation of its ideas through personal sacrifice."*

No less complicated was the preparation of the works of Bruckner, notably, all of the Symphonies. Neglia presented these works in Hamburg between 1910 and 1914 in a series of memorable performances, which were reviewed by Edward Neill in a contribution published by the Italian Association "A. Bruckner."

"... Performing in Hamburg to work as hard as the Third Bruckner by an Italian director is the most extraordinary performance that could happen.

Even more extraordinary is the fact that the executions of Bruckneriane works by Italian conductors are so rare that you can easily count them on one hand. The example of Neglia is to debunk the myth that wants to make Bruckner a "genius loci" understandable only by the Austrians and by the Germans, and we clearly demonstrate that the sensitivity of an Italian artist can open up to Bruckner more difficult and in seemingly inaccessible. Especially since, as a glance at the concert programs of the Hamburg Neglia, we note that already in 1911, he showed that work so complex difficult and even for the Germans themselves, which is the Ninth Symphony in D Minor."

After a performance of Bruckner's ninth, on January 31, a glowing review defines Neglia's understanding of the intrinsic nature and the spirit of the symphony. Neglia is honestly and sincerely one with the value and love of music:

"Francesco Paolo Neglia, the brave artist, continues to fight with courage. The inner impulse of his nature throughout reaching to the artistic activity and the intimate, compelling needs of his soul, which is music became only, the categorical imperative of his life. He leads the performance, directs the orchestra and gives concerts even if it cost him great sacrifices. He is, therefore, a real idealist."

Even in that distant land after the years of war where he lived between hardship and misfortune, he devoted himself almost exclusively to teaching music. Giulio Confalonieri, critic, and musicologist of Milan wrote that Neglia *"was the first Italian composer who opened the discussion on the coexistence of melodrama Mediterranean with Wagnerian experience."*

Francesco Paolo Neglia

Neglia's Musical Output

<u>Working for Orchestra</u>
Symphonies:
- 1901 *Fine Sinfonia in Re minor (Symphony in D minor)*
- 1912 *Sinfonia no.2 - Symphony "The emigrant" for* large orchestra

Other works for orchestra
- 1896 *Intermezzo Breve*, for orchestra
- 1898 *Due Rispetti*, for strings, harp, and organ
- 1913 *Suite Sinfonica "Tre Quadri di vita Veneziana"* for orchestra, op. 32
- *Arioso*, for strings, harp, timpani and harmonium, op. 17
- *Danza fantastic*
- *Gavot*, for string orchestra
- *Largo*, for strings, harp, and organ
- *Minuetto in Stile Antico*, for string orchestra, op. 14
- *Pizzicato Gavot*, for string orchestra
- *Prelude*
- *Serenata Siciliana*, for string orchestra, op. 37
- *Sinfonietta*, for orchestra, op. 31

Working for Banda
- 1896 *Parata d'Eroi*, large military march for banda
- *Adagio from the symphony "De emigrant,"* for banda
- *Fantasia Eroica*, for banda op. 33
- *Minuetto in Stile Antico*, for banda op. 14

Masses and Other Church Music
- 1896 *Inno a Santa Anna*, for soloists, mixed choir, and orchestra
- 1916 *Due Canzoncine Religioso*, for voice and string quartet, op. 65
- 1916 *Due Canzoncine Religioso*, for two voices and organ, op. 65
- *Ave Maria*, for voice, violin and piano, op. 10
- *Ave Maria*, for four voices, op. 36
- *Ave Maria*, for two voices and organ, op. 12
- *Compieta Maggiore*, for voice and organ, op. 67
- *Gloria in Excelsis Deo*, five-part fugue
- *Missa Brevis*, for tenors, basses, and organ (or: small orchestra), op. 34
- *Responsorio per la Settimana Santa*, for baritone and organ, op. 35
- *Tantum Ergo*, op. 66

Music Theater
Opera
- Zelia, op. 78

Operette
- 1927 Girifalco

Vocal Music
Working for choir
- *Canto Popular*, for mixed choir
- *As that flower*, Madrigal for soprano (or tenor) and piano
- *Campane*, for four voices, op. 84
- *Il Saluto di Beatrice*, for mezzo-soprano and piano, op. 25
- *La Canzone*, for soprano, contra-alto, tenor and bass, op. 21

- *Litania*, for two voices and piano, op. 63
- *Nations of harmony*, for basses and voices (collection of songs and hymns for children)

  1. Inno alla Bandiera "I tre colori", op. 41 - text: Cavallotti
  2. Campana, op. 50
  3. Inno scolastico, op. 55
  4. Coro di Pastorelle, op. 53
  5. Il Ritorno alla terra, op. 54
  6. Il Grillino, op. 47
  7. Giro Tondo, op. 69

- *Quannu*, for tenor and piano, op. 2
- *Sepulto Domino*, for tenor, bass, violin, cello and organ, op. 68
- *Sfinge*, Lirica for baritone and piano, op. 48
- *Sphynx*, romance for voice and piano

Chamber Music
- *Bagattella*, for violin, flute, horn and piano, op. 24
- *Caprice waltz*, for violin and piano
- *Idyl*, for violin and piano
- *Interlude*, for violin and piano
- *Largo Espressivo*, for violin and piano, op. 40
- *Minuet*, for violin and piano
- *Minuet*, for cello and piano
- *Old-fashioned Sonata*, for violin and piano
- *Quartet*, for violin, viola, cello and piano
- *Romance*, for cello and piano
- *Sicilian Serenade*, for violin and piano
- *Trio*, for violin, cello and piano, op. 52

Working for Organ
- *Ave Maria*, op. 8
- *Nostalgia (Homesickness)*, op. 16
- *L'Arpista Fantastico*, op. 38
- *Major Compieta*

Working for Piano
- *Sonatina in un Tempo*, op. 11
- *Scherzo*
- *Sicilian Serenade*, op. 17
- *Youthful remembrances*
- *Siete canto popolare*

Working for Mandolin
- *Fantasia*, for mandolin solo, op. 6

Additionally, he wrote two educational books: *Theoretical and Practical Harmony* and *Appendix to the Notions of Harmony*.

Scuola Elementare F.P. Neglia - Enna, Sicily

Venice

"Serendipity was my tour guide, assisted by caprice" ~Pico Iyer

August 14, Day 7 - Venice and the Tronchetto, 351 kilometers

Apart from the excitement of our next destination, the nearly four-hour ride was uneventful. I found the A4 was a bit dull and flat, something we had not experienced thus far on the trip. It was the complete opposite of the rolling hills and grandeur of the mountains.

By the time we saw the first road sign for Venice, and the parking area, Il Tronchetto, my excitement began to rise. It had been nearly 20 years since my last visit to Venice.

The Tronchetto is a large parking structure, placed on a human-made island, just southwest of the island of Venice itself. There are six levels to the structure, and the cost to park is only €21 per day, making the building both a convenient and economical choice

If there was only one thing that concerned me about our entire 16-day experience, it was this very issue; how to get from the Tronchetto with all of our luggage to The Hotel Antiche Figure.

The signs for the Tronchetto directed us to take the next exit and turn right into the entrance. We proceeded to climb to the very top of the structure, parking on the fifth level in row D.

Once outside the Tronchetto, we had to find the way to the hotel. Many people were walking along the northern side of the walkway and we decided to follow them. After about 100 steps, I saw a woman getting into her parked car, which was in a designated parking area. She was probably a native, so I decided to ask her how to get to the city limits. She informed me that, for only one euro each, we could take the shuttle two stops to I termini, in Venice proper. I thanked her and proceeded to take the walkway to the right, then straight into the building directly in front of us.

On the second floor of the building was a ramp which would take us to the waiting shuttle. We boarded the shuttle and while we waited to leave, were able to read a sign which told us the first stop was where the cruise ships dock. The second stop was for all those who were on the cruise ships which were docked for the day and wanted to enjoy the sights of Venice. The second stop was the central train station, and the final stop was where we would disembark.

Instead of dragging our luggage from I termini to our hotel, I thought it would be nice to treat my family to a private water taxi ride. I asked the first driver I saw, "Quanto costa portarci all'Hotel Antiche Figure?" He laughed and said, "It would cost about 25€ for what we can walk in five minutes. Just follow the walkway for 200 meters, and you will arrive." After thanking him, we followed his instructions, climbed over two small bridges, and came to the entrance of our new home for the next three nights.

We checked into the rather small, but very charming, Hotel Figure. I chose this hotel because it was a 20-or-so minute walk to the touristy areas of the Rialto Bridge, The Bridge of Sighs and Piazza San Marco. I hoped it would be more peaceful than the hotels closer to the more touristy locations were. Besides, we enjoy walking.

Although we were somewhat exhausted followed by the long drive and the parking episode, we mustered up the energy to go exploring. However, instead of challenging ourselves to the long walk to St. Marco, we chose not to go as far and to explore our surroundings close to the hotel.

Twenty meters to the right of our hotel was a bridge which would take us in the direction of the major attractions. As previously agreed, we opted to stay on the south side of the bridge and do some exploring closer to home.

We walked and walked, and walked and walked; crossing bridge after bridge, we made rights, lefts, and crossed more bridges, continued straight until we crossed another bridge. Through all of this traipsing, we lost our total collective sense of direction and also worked up quite an appetite, as we hadn't eaten since leaving Stresa earlier in the day.

We stumbled upon a place which had an enormous zuppa de pesce on display near the front window. This meal wasn't a large bowl of fish, but a huge tureen which held a minimum of 20 pounds of fish, pasta, and broth. We took our seats around the waiting table.

We all ordered different dishes and shared a fork or spoonful with each other. I told the waiter as I was pointing to the pot, please, bring me *that* along with a carafe of the house red. The red was just what the doctor ordered; the meal was sublime in every way imaginable. A delicious overflowing bowl of zuppa de pesce, our feet resting, minds free from all responsibilities of the day, the car was parked, and most importantly, we were in one of the most amazing cities in the world.

After our hearty meal, we continued to see all of the sights. We were still lost, or shall I say, without any real sense of direction, but no one seemed to be concerned.

We visited many touristy knick-knack stores, as well as an incredible produce stand. We procured a bushel of small, ripe tomatoes, for later consumption. Just up the block from the vegetable stand was the most exquisite family-owned European deli.

Although still stuffed from our most recent meal, we made our purchases: 50 grams of prosciutto, 50 grams of mortadella, 100 grams of fresh cheese from the region, and some crusty bread stuffed with olives.

As we meandered the streets, I noticed one of the bridges looked very familiar to me. It was the same one we crossed when we first entered the city, just past the water taxi stand. We were home.

We sat in our room for about an hour, took a nice hot shower, soaked our feet, and watched Amadeus in Italian, the uncut version. The movie was a perfect nightcap to a long, exhausting, yet beautiful day with my family.

After staring at each other for a few minutes, our silence spoke volumes, we opened the waiting bottle of wine and enjoyed a relaxing glass before turning down the covers.

GBP Saga

"The harder the conflict, the more glorious the triumph."
~Thomas Paine

In April of 2016, an old friend of mine sent me an email, wanting to reconnect. She told me that she would be performing a show at the New Jersey Performing Arts Center the following November. She was hoping that we could get together to catch up on the past 20 years while she was in town.

After checking my schedule, I shared with her that on the same day, November 13, I had a performance in New Brunswick at the State Theater at 3 p.m. It was too bad that I had another engagement, as it would have been nice to see each other after all this time.

I jotted another email and asked Amy what time her performance began on the 13th, which she informed me was at 7 p.m. My show was scheduled to end around 5:15 and I figured I could be at the NJPAC by 6:00.

After firming up our plans, I thought to myself, "Amy is performing in my hall, and it seemed to me that she was conducting an event which required an orchestra." I decided to email her again and ask her directly if she needed an orchestra for her show? "Yes, I do," she replied, "Perhaps you know someone who can secure the orchestra for me?" I chuckled while writing back, sharing with her the other hat that I've worn for all of these years, as an orchestra contractor. I asked Any to put me in touch with the managing director of the tour.

Over the next few days, I found the exact requirements needed for The Legend of Zelda show. The production requires a 56-piece orchestra, as well as a 20-member chorus. Additionally, the complete back line of percussion and timpani required a rental.

I Googled "Legend of Zelda," and came across the current 2016 tour, which included all of the upcoming dates and venues on the tour. Emailing my friend, I asked, who was in charge of the entire operation of the tour; I learned was Giovanni Batista, the owner of GMP Live.

I sent him an email as a form of introduction. Giovanni responded as a true professional would, offering to get together to talk about working together. By that time, he had already accepted me as Amy's referral, as well as my bid for the performance at the NJPAC in November; Giovanni knew I was the real deal. Now, I needed to impress upon him he needed to secure me as GBP Live's tour coordinator.

We agreed to meet at Pizzante at 69 West 55th Street in New York City, to discuss a possible collaboration for all the remaining North American tour dates, while we shared a meal.

When we entered the restaurant and the maître d' saw Giovanni, it was as if Moses was parting the Red Sea. All eyes in the room focused on him. People came rushing over to greet and welcome us both to the restaurant.

We were escorted upstairs to what appeared to be his regular table. I was feeling very special and honored to be part of this extraordinary experience.

When the waiter arrived at our table, there was no English exchanged; this was a strictly Italian celebration. The waiter asked me "Cosa ti va da bere?" or "What would you like to drink?" I responded, and Giovanni smiled at my understanding of the language. Although my language skills are decent, I have spent more than the past decade listening to and understanding Russian as that is my wife's native tongue. Consequently, my Italian language was rusty, at best.

Not wanting to waste Giovanni's time, I had looked at the online menu the night before our meeting. When Giovanni asked me what I would like, I was prepared with an answer. I told him I was going to get like the polpo alla Mediterranean – grilled Mediterranean octopus, olives, mashed potatoes, and roasted tomatoes with lemon dressing. His response was priceless; he exclaimed, "That is what I am ordering!"

I felt that we were heading in the right direction already and was more than hopeful that we would strike up a deal. Before the food came, I explained my position to Giovanni: if he secured me as his music coordinator for the North American performances, it would allow him to focus on gaining new bookings or other pressing matters.

Being a good businessman, he asked me what my fee would be to lighten his burden. I shared my number. He began computing, and within just a few seconds, agreed. We spoke, briefly about an agreement, but we both realized that a formal agreement was not needed. Instead, Giovanni extended his right hand to mine and with that, we had our contract.

A handshake is a very old Italian statement of trust, which is stronger than written words, as it is an agreement of honor. We both agreed and continued our conversation which now moved to our homeland, family, enjoyment of life and much more in the personal field.

Leaving the restaurant, we walked out together through the front entrance onto the street. Giovanni asked where I had parked my car, and I told him my car was right next door about 10 feet away. We chatted about our newly formed alliance but also about something more important: our family lives, and love of our heritage. With that, I invited him to my home for Sunday dinner. Sunday is the most sacred of all days in Italian culture and for me to even suggest a gathering on a Sunday was, in effect, extending my arms around him and his family without moving a muscle. That was all I needed to solidify the deal and our new-found friendship. What a remarkable turn of events.

June 8, 2:37:12 p.m.
A few months have passed. I have been busy booking various local contractors to take care of our needs throughout the region. I am working with contractors from Fresno to Oklahoma City, and from Houston to Louisville, 19 cities in all.

While filing contracts with each local contractor, I recall one of them suggested that they would prefer to receive a deposit up-front and the final payment before the event took place. This seemed odd to me, as all other contractors are accepting company checks on the day of the performance, or direct payment from the venue.

I set myself on a mission to understand the reasoning behind this request and discover if there was any justification for accepting it.

On June 21, 2016, I called The Local musicians union, to see if there was any information I could learn about my new client. After learning about an alleged internal dispute, it was time to call Giovanni and learn what happened from his perspective. He, after paying his contractor in full, he felt he had nothing more to do.

The Local wanted the issue to be solved in order to make good on the original deal, and Giovanni felt nothing is owed. Now, I am stuck in the middle.

As of now, both parties seem to be at odds, neither willing to budge. Giovanni can continue business as usual, and The Local continues to be angry by what they perceive as his arrogance. The truth is, Giovanni doesn't need to be taken off the unfair list in order to operate. If any local contractor is uncomfortable that GBP is on the unfair list, GBP can pay the complete cost up front, along with the fully executed contract.

My responsibility is to resolve this issue for both my client and union. I believe in a musician's rights, union protection, health & welfare, and pension contributions, all of which are benefits of being a union member.

While considering both sides of this story, I needed to dig deeper to get more clarity. Something didn't add up.

There were many discrepancies between the two stories. Firstly, there weren't 100 orchestra members needed for the Barclays Center; only 56 were required for the performance. Another problem facing us was disbursement, even if Giovanni did pay the additional fee, how was the Local going to distribute the money amongst the orchestra members? In a prior conversation, I had learned that there was no contract, therefore no list of participating orchestra members. I was now armed with some compelling points to share with the Local that could aid in a successful resolution.

On June 28, 2016, I received a call from The Local, informing me that they were lowering GBP Live's obligation by over 75%. After thanking the Local for the reduction, I felt the price was still too high. I couldn't help but wonder where that money would go since The Local could not apply it towards salaries, nor pension payments for the musicians.

I called the Local to show them support. During this conversation, I also came up with several ideas on how we may be able to proceed. One of which was for me to personally ensure the Local and Federation that this type of circumstance will never happen again, as long as I am working for the company. I shared with them that I had just started working with GBP and would make sure that they are compliant in all venues throughout North America, going forward. In fact, I would be willing to sign of a three-year contract with the Federation touring department, indicating that GBP will abide by the touring agreement at the Federation and Local guidelines I was banking that my 30-year relationship and reputation with the Local and Federation would help sway all parties.

During my phone call with GBP, we shared a very candid discussion about how to proceed. I gently pushed Giovanni to see the benefits of a good working relationship with the Federation and all locals. We decided that he would sign an agreement with the Federation Touring Department, but would not pay them their requested fee as a punishment.

Because I have been down this road before, I was able to draw on laws that govern such acts and remember that it is illegal in the state of New York to find a person or entity for such matters. An employer is able to suspend an employee, but not fine or garnish their wages under the current law.

Because neither the Federation nor the Local Union has a mechanism in place for implementing fines, I came up with an alternate idea. GBP can make a donation to the Musicians Emergency Relief Fund (ERF), which relies on the charitable contributions of members and those who support working musicians. The ERF is a non-profit organization, and all donations are tax-deductible.

I thought that this could be a perfect solution if we could come to a consensus on the donation amount. The Local was firm at their bid but felt that half of that amount was a fair middle-ground.

After a half dozen phone calls with The Local and the Federation, we began to share the same vision. It was our collective duty to share our proposal with the President of The Local, and it was my task to get Giovanni to agree. We both set out to do our best and decided to touch base before the end of the day.

At 4:07 p.m., I received an agreement from The Local, who agreed to the terms and to squash their beef with GDP, once Giovanni signed the contract and made the donation.

The next day, I sent Giovanni the following email:

Tuesday, June 28 at 10:34 a.m.
I have worked very hard on this offer and hope you will find it acceptable. It is in our best interest to resolve this matter as seamlessly as possible.

You will be in good standing if you become a signatory to Federation touring contract; this means that you will continue to hire union orchestras in the US and Canada. Also, make a $2500 donation to the Musicians Emergency Relief Fund. This donation is 100% deductible as they are a 501(c)(3).

I am working with the Federation on getting the touring contract in place. Once I have it, and you have had a chance to review and sign it, the union and Federation will move to take you off the unfair list. The proper order would be to sign the contract first and then make the contribution. Buonanotte e parlare presto!

I expect that Giovanni will accept the offer. He knows that I have used my reputation with The Local, as well as the Federation, to broker this deal. He is aware of the politics involved in my decision making and why I had pushed so hard. Sharing this story chapter is intended to pay tribute to The Local, the Federation, and Giovanni Battista for working together to find common ground, something that rarely takes place.

Low and behold, three days later he accepted the offer!

The Federation enclosed the new version of the agreement in their follow-up email, which contained all of my negotiated terms, terms I felt would be acceptable to my new client and forwarded to Giovanni straight away. I wanted to see this agreement move forward for several reasons, with the most important reason being how this it would solidify my position with GBP as their North American Music Coordinator. Beyond that, I felt the agreement would take GBP off of the International unfair list and would offer me, a proverbial feather in my negotiating cap.

An article appeared in the International Musicians Newspaper which reads in part:

Legend of Zelda Employers
Pledge Union Agreement

"The concert production The Legend of Zelda-Symphony of the Goddesses, has two separate employers producing various dates in the US and Canada in 2016 and early 2017, GBP has been removed from the AFM's "Unfair List." They will, therefore, file proper AFM local union contracts for all upcoming bookings.

GBP has engaged Jim Neglia of The Local as a national orchestra coordinator for all their engagements. Neglia is working with local unions and local contractors to ensure all GBP dates are covered properly."

I impressed upon both The Local and the Federation how important it would be to recognize, in their newspaper, the role I played in the resolution between two parties. My years of experience and talents in defusing situations, and my desire to remain apolitical, allowed me to find the proper balance between all involved.

Feeling fantastic about the outcome of the events of the past weeks, I decided to open a bottle of Sassicaia 2010. I was waiting for a good reason to open this particular bottle and felt this was a good enough reason to pull the cork. While sipping, I Googled Sassicaia 2010 and found the following description:

"This supremely elegant and age-worthy Sassicaia opens with an intense bouquet of black cherry, Mediterranean herbs, blue flower, cedar and leather aromas. Powerful but graceful, the palate delivers a vibrant core of black cherry accented with white pepper, mineral and balsamic notes alongside youthful but polished tannins and vibrant acidity."

Saluti, proprio quello che il dottore ha ordinato! (Greetings, just what the doctor ordered!)

The Venetian Lagoon

"Life is a magical journey, so travel endlessly to unfold its profound and heart touching beauty." ~Debasish Mridha

August 15, Day 8, Murano, Burano and Isola San Michele

After a deep, peaceful rest; I awoke. Everyone was still asleep when I left the hotel room and headed downstairs to see what was waiting in the breakfast area.

Thus far, each day of our trip, I have visited the breakfast area early and alone, my only accompaniment being my trusty journal, pencil, eraser, and sharpener. I take great pleasure in writing down what I was experiencing during yesterday's travels and reflections on how I felt after my experiences. There were times, especially today, where I felt like I was living as I did all those years ago, writing, preparing chapters for a book I have yet to write. It felt great to be back in my old routine.

Because my family was with me on this trip, documenting my experiences was even more enjoyable. Old habits of documenting, coupled with my love of European culture embraces me, even more, this time around. The love I feel, the desires I have, the need to share, and reward this time, and a deeper understanding of what I am doing.

An hour or so passed before my family appeared at the entrance of the dining room, to join me for a well-deserved breakfast. As they were finishing their meal, I was making arrangements with the front desk for a taxi ride to the island of Murano.

Transportation to any of the islands was something the hotel offered as a complimentary service to their guests. There must have been an excellent agreement between Morano and all the hotels on the Island of Venice, as we were about to find out that it is nearly impossible to visit Morano without making a purchase. The "free" taxi rides cost Morano little, but they could charge the vacationer a hefty sum.

At the appointed time the taxi arrived and we, along with two other women, made the 20-minute journey to the Isola di Morano. The water ride to Morano was both beautiful and exhilarating. A brisk pace, jumping the waves helped open my senses to the beauty of the trip. Time seemingly stood still. I looked all around and absorbed every detail before my eyes. The soft ripple of the water spilling onto the city barriers, Saint Mark's Campanile cutting through the landscape, the bronze sculpture of The Barque of Dante which sat in the middle of the canal, and just the general calmness in the air showered me with warmth.

Once on the Island, we disembarked and entered the glass factory. Once inside, we witnessed a quick demonstration on how to blow a glass vase, as well as a more complex horse creation. After the presentation, we entered the main showroom, which was filled with chandeliers, lamps, figurines, vases, fish bowls, tea sets and more, there were endless rooms filled with master artists work.

As we passed from room to room, my son Phillip spotted a decorative picture of the city of Venice. I couldn't help but notice as he gazed at the piece, as he then tried to walk away, but couldn't, he stood mesmerized. The image was a specialty craft of Morano, in which the artist would take any picture and press it in gold leaf. Once in the leaf, they would affix the image to the glass, through a process which was foreign to me. The final product was an incredible landscape of multicolored, multifaceted beauty.

Depending on your viewing position, the angle, and the light, one can see a completely different piece of art. Looking at the price of nearly 7000 €, I knew it was above my comfort zone, even though I can see the beauty and artistry of the work. A salesperson saw we took a liking to the work and informed us that he could reduce the price by 50% or 3500 €. Still, even with the generous discount, it was above my budget, so I declined. Taking a deep breath, I recognized the value of the piece and began to consider the offer of 3500 € again. The price for the originality alone seemed worth it to me. Plus, I couldn't take my eyes off of the picture.

We continued walking through the gallery, admiring all of the items produced in glass. Roughly 15 minutes later, the owner of the shop appeared. The salesperson who had been working with us explained to him how much we appreciate and related to the arts. We shared with him that Sasha and I were classical musicians with a major symphony orchestra back in the United States.

We spoke a great deal, and the genuine conversation seemed to make an impact on the owner of the establishment as it did for us. In spite of my weak Italian skills, and his lack of the English, we recognized our universal love of art, music, and family.

His new offer for the gold leaf was a 70% reduction of the original price. I was nearly prepared to purchase the piece at a 50% off, so it wasn't the most difficult decision I've had to make in my life. I couldn't possibly consider letting this picture go.

Years before, I was performing on an Italian tour. While in Florence, a friend came across two gorgeous leather jackets, one brown and the other black. He asked me, which one he should get, to which I responded by asking him the following "If you were to purchase both, would it put you in a different tax bracket?" He laughed, understanding my message, and purchased both.

I felt like this was my leather jacket decision and confirmed the purchase partially on the advice I gave all those years ago.

There were many factors which lead to my ultimate acceptance of this beautiful work of art. Supporting the artist, loving the piece, but most importantly was the excitement on Phillips' face when we pulled the trigger to make the purchase. A priceless moment!

The idea of purchasing a 24-carat gold inlay picture on the Island or Morano, a place I was likely never to return in my lifetime, made all the sense in the world. I remember my wife commented to the salesman on the level of intricacy in the picture saying "The amount of detail to produce such a work of art is unbelievable." "If you feel that way, you should consider making this an unforgettable purchase," he responded. He was good, and his words rang true in our ears. He was also one of the master glass-smiths in Morano with more than 30 years of experience producing his craft. That to us, counted for something.

While paying for the picture, the clerk asked us, "Where we would like to go next? Our boats will take you anywhere you desire." With limited knowledge, we tossed back the question to him and asked if he could offer some suggestions." The immediate response was "Burano, no question."

Without asking for any further detail, we agreed and stepped outside. With the receipt in my pocket, we made our way to the waiting boat. A short 15-minute trip took us further north to the pastel island of Burano, where we spent the next four hours in absolute heaven.

We soon learned that Burano was considered the most beautiful of all the Venetian Islands. At first, I was a bit skeptical, but shortly after arriving at the tiny island, I was convinced. I knew that Burano was famous for their production of lace and that Leonardo da Vinci visited in the latter part of the 15th century. He purchased a lace cloth for the main altar of Il Duomo in Milano, and soon, lace exports across Europe were booming.

As we got off the boat, the first thing that we noticed was that the façade of each house was painted a clean, calming pastel color. There is a peacefulness in the air, a mellowing, calming vibe of the city. We immediately felt the charming and embracing effects she had on us.

The other noticeable aspect of Burano were the countless lace and jewelry shops in the area where everything is Morano made. There were glass necklaces, bracelets, rings and earrings of every sort, every color, and every design imaginable.

Having made a significant purchase just a short time ago, then taking the exciting trip in the boat on the Venice waterway, our appetites were triggered. It was time for a bite to eat. There were so many options, so many restaurants surrounding us, we had a difficult time choosing where to go. After walking for a few blocks, we came across a restaurant that bragged to be the only family-run establishment on the island of Burano. Plus, they offered free Wi-Fi. How could we say no?

We ordered grilled cuttlefish, thin noodles with crab sauce, muscles in crab sauce, and a large salad, which was accompanied by half carafe of house rosé. We were all content with the delicious meal, peaceful atmosphere, and superb service.

After our stomachs were filled, we pushed on. We scoured the shops for memories we could take back home, as souvenirs of our travels. I found two sets of glass cufflinks that I thought would look handsome with my white tuxedo shirt, one black with red highlights, and another white stone with golden and yellow highlights. I decided to treat myself to this excellent gift.

I will always remember Morano as a magical location. I am not sure I will ever visit a place that will even come close to its splendor. I genuinely felt completely at peace, and at home here.

It was time to head back to the mainland of Venice. We no longer had the use of the private shuttle afforded us in Morano, so this time, we had to use public transportation; Il Vaporetto!

Although this is perhaps the least expensive mode of transportation in all of Venice, there is one downside— they pack you on the Vaporetto like sardines.

Under normal circumstances, the proximity would have been bearable, except that it was a blistering 34° outside. We were packed on the boat with little to no breeze, which made our travel much less comfortable. We all decided that we needed to do our best to ignore the heat and sweaty neighbors and enjoy whatever our current surrounding threw at us.

Looking at the map, we saw that we were nine stops away from the Isole San Michele, home of the famous Venetian Cemetery. From Burano, we took the Number 1 until were reached the transfer spot. The softly spoken boatman confirmed the stop, and we waited for the Number 41 to arrive, which would ultimately take us to the cemetery.

After a few minutes ride, we found ourselves at our final stop of the day. Upon our arrival, we felt it was worth every ounce of sweat to be in such a revered place.

Just outside of the cemetery was a precise map of the resting place of all the souls in this dignified space. I sought out the master himself and memorized his location. The map indicated area 61, near the center of the cemetery.

We made our way through each passageway, following the stone walkway from one area to the next. When we arrived at area 61, the first thing that struck me was the size of the area, which was smaller than expected. I had anticipated seeing a significant, ornate tomb, but nothing in the area caught my eye. We passed some big stones, many carved with meticulous decorative craftsmanship. I wondered what the grave marker would look like for the great Igor Stravinsky.

We read names and dates on the row closest to us, which featured stones that dated back to those born in 1820 and departure dates as late as 1998. The further we walked, the more I found myself falling into a reflective mood.

As we passed the south wall, we turned left, headed straight, then made a right on the most northern side of area 61. The headstones were of varying sizes and styles, all different in aesthetic. Some of the headstones were made from concrete, while others from marble.

Moving down the back row of the area, just a few more paces, we came upon grave marker #36 and next to Igor was his wife Vera at marker #37. Their graves were simple, not ornate as I had imagined, each three by six-foot slabs of white marble which listed only their names. No mention of their greatness, his genius, nothing at all.

I thought to myself how fitting it was for him to have such a plain marker: it was the absolute antithesis of his music and all it represents. His incredibly complex compositions, his scoring abilities, his use of rhythmic intensity, integrated harmonies, his use of an augmented orchestra, all of that with no mention of music anywhere near his burial place.

After I was finished examining their graves, I placed a small stone on the corner of his and Vera's plaques, in honor of their memories.

While heading back to our hotel, this thought resounded in my head; s we move through life, we change things slightly and leave our mark behind, however small or large. In return, as the days tick by, life leaves her marks on us as well.

Back at the Hotel Antiche Figure, it is now 21:20, and I am feeling peaceful and extremely content, after a long day. Phillip, Daniel, and Sasha just left for a walk around the city, while I am heading out to sit by the water and write, once again breaking my morning writing ritual. Once outside, I ordered a glass of wine.

Tomorrow we depart for Croatia, where I have learned the fantastic weather awaiting us is 33°- 34° C, with 10 miles per hour breeze and zero percent chance of rain. It is amazingly comfortable sitting here in these Venetian surroundings, writing down my thoughts, while sipping this heavenly

Chianti. In the distance, I can hear the Vaporetto moving up and down the waterway, their humming motors, part of the distinct Venice charm.

As I put the empty wine glass down on the table, I lifted my head to see my family approaching. It was time for bed.

Grave of Igor and Vera Stravinsky

The Night Before

"It is a shame for a man to grow old without seeing the beauty
and strength of which his body is capable." ~Socrates

Journal entry: February 11, 2017 11:42 p.m.

What is it that Chuck would say in times like this? "Head down, eyes
straight forward and focus!" How I miss him. I didn't think I would say
that, especially at this stage in my life and career. Nevertheless, here I am,
left eye twitching uncontrollably – deep in thought, needing his guidance.

Most would feel on top of the world, to have so much in life: so much
work, so much happiness, and a promising future yet to come. This year,
thousands of musicians are working, due to my efforts with various North
American tours, and that is a great feeling. Although there is a productive
amount of activity flying all about, I am feeling unworthy, lacking energy,
and just plain old low. I am having difficulty separating the 'contractor
and personnel manager; me from the "other," more personal, me, as a
husband and father.

In the past, when I wore all of my hats, I did it with relative ease. Why is it
posing an issue, now? I believe I know the answer. I am no longer excited

about working solely as a personnel manager with a symphony, and as a result, I struggle with all that it implies.

Considering my degenerative hearing loss, I struggle at times to perform. Should I leave my symphony job and move to work for other organizations? Should I work for for-profit groups, where hearing is less of a need? Should I leave the symphony now, while I am still able to contribute, or do I wait until I completely embarrass myself over my lack of hearing? I don't know if am ready for this transition. These are the nagging questions running through my mind this evening.

When considering the gratifying side of my contracting career, there is the raw excitement of not knowing who will call or email me with the next project. Perhaps I will work on a repeat project with the multi-billion-dollar company *NIKE,* or perhaps it will be with Michelin Manufacturing Company again, or maybe fashion guru Michael Kors and the New York fashion show? Would it be from another video game corporation who wants to take me on as their music coordinator for North America, or any of a million other possibilities?

I began feeling such undue pressure over my thinking, such a feeling of complete and utter distress. I needed to dig deep into my bag of tricks to start pulling myself from the depths of absolute despair. I feel tormented. I had no one to attribute my feelings to, but myself.

I put myself on a path of uncertainty, which is a stark contrast to the kind of life I have been living all these years, as a secure successful career with the symphony. However, I knew that I desired so much more than the symphony could offer. To add to the complexities of my thinking, I had for the first time in nearly 50 years, the means to make the transition. The profit companies were now seeking my services. I needed to accept this change and abandon all my fears, perhaps extracting myself from the current.

But what a humiliation for me when someone standing next to me heard a flute in the distance, and I heard nothing, or someone standing next to me heard a shepherd singing and again I heard nothing. Such incidents drove me almost to despair; a little more of that and I would have ended my life - it was only my art that held me back.

~Ludwig van Beethoven

Since 2013, I have suffered dramatically from the dreaded disease of tinnitus. Tinnitus affects my sense of hearing, as I cannot hear what I am playing, completely. I think I can feel what is happening, but in reality, I cannot be sure. The entirety upper range of my hearing is no longer functional.

At the onset of this horrible disease a few years back, I was asked to perform a series of recording sessions which would later produce a CD release. One selection that we recorded is the William Tell Overture of Gioachino Rossini, to which I was assigned the triangle part. The triangle part happens to be one of the most beautifully written in the literature.

In the pastoral section of this work, a Ranz des Vaches or "Call to the cows," signals the calm after the storm. This passage features the English horn alternating phrases with the flute, culminating in a duet with the triangle that accompanies them in the background.

For this soft, lyrical section, I chose to use my newly purchased Buddy & Thein seven-inch triangle. This particular instrument not only offered a solid tone but a beautiful spread of that specific sound. It is almost like the note would vibrate, all by itself.

The ending of the pastoral requires the percussionist to play a pianissimo triangle roll. Because I use a larger (in diameter) beater for the single notes, there was no time to change beaters before the magical soft tremolo. Consequently, I was forced to dig deep to create the exact sound which was in my mind. Using a medium-sized beater, I was able to control the complete dynamic range required for the opening of the work.

Once we had completed the entire recording, the contractor called a 20-minute break for the orchestra. During the break, the recording engineer welcomed me to the production studio to listen to my beautiful sound produced during the pastoral section. I was looking forward to a beautiful experience

When I entered the recording booth, the engineer placed headphones over my head. As the passage was approaching, I waited with genuine excitement to hear my contribution.

That did not happen. Instead, the music played in my headset, and during the solo section he was so excited to share with me, I heard what my ears would allow, which was nothing, whatsoever. Not a single note, not a sound, not even a glimpse into how I sounded. At that moment, I knew my career as an orchestral percussionist might be coming to an end.

Opatija and Trieste

"That's the place to get to—nowhere. One wants to wander away from the world's somewheres, into our own nowhere" ~D.H. Lawrence

August 16 - Day 9 Opatija, Croatia, 240 Kilometers

This particular drive was exhilarating for me. I couldn't wait to get into the car and begin the trek to Trieste. I was interested in seeing this northern Italian city for many reasons, one being that it was at a geographical junction where Italy, Slovenia, and Croatia all meet. A stone's throw in any direction and you would hit another country. Another reason to visit Trieste: it is the city where my father was born. Naturally, I was curious to explore the town.

As we approached our destination, we noticed that there was nothing remotely the same about Trieste and Venice. Apart from the obvious, the city was clean with little or no graffiti and featured open squares with very few people occupying the piazzas. In the center of the city was Piazza Unità d'Italia. This Piazza was among the largest I have ever seen, rivaling the enormity of Plaza Mayor in Madrid. A little gem stuck in northern Italy.

Trieste, it is the capital of the autonomous region Friuli-Venezia Giulia and the Trieste province. The city sits towards the end of a narrow strip of Italian territory lying between the Adriatic Sea and Slovenia, which lies almost immediately south and east of the city. We found Trieste to be unexpectedly gorgeous.

Hungry from our journey, we stopped at a "Panini" establishment, where you could create your own sandwich with a salami and cheese base, with an extensive menu of add-ons. We enjoyed several varieties, including a tasty ham and cheese with oregano and another with fresh tomatoes.

We spent a few short hours milling about, walking around the Piazza, and throughout the side streets. The city had a warm and welcoming feeling, one which sat well with me. I did question if the embracing sense had anything to do with Trieste being the birthplace of my father, as I am not sure I can separate the city from that emotion.

When we began our walk back to our parked car, we passed through the grand piazza once again. In doing so, we passed many outdoor tables which were now mostly occupied by feasting locals. Before our very eyes, we witnessed a sight that would become the topic of conversation for the rest of the day.

There were a man and a woman who was being served at one of the tables. As the waiter placed the first plate of food on the table top, a large group of pigeons swooped in for a taste. It was like a picture out of Alfred Hitchcock's The Birds—absolute violence occurred. Dozens of pigeons landed on the table; rather, they landed on the newly placed plate of food.

No matter how many times the waiter slapped his dish towel on the table, the pigeons would not retreat. In fact, they seemed to become more determined in their action, with every swat. The waiter then placed the second plate of food down, to try to frighten the birds once and for all, but it didn't help at all. More pigeons joined in the feast, coming out of nowhere, converging on the plates. It was a smorgasbord of delight for what appeared to be a party for 30 or more pigeons.

The meals were devoured by the pigeon's, the drinks on the table were toppled over, glass shattering on the cobblestones below. Even with all the commotion, the pigeons never let up. They had a tenacious "New York" attitude about them. My mind then turned my memories to the motorcyclists we encountered at the start of our trip in Stresa; they feared nothing. Was it the motorcyclists who learned from the birds? That is completely possible.

Once we managed to get back on the road, we soon approached the Italian border. I was sure we would head directly into Croatia, but much to my surprise, we came upon the Italian-Slovenia border control.

We always have our passports prepared for all crossing, but rarely have had to use them; today was different. The border guard collected all four of our passports, gave the car a once over, and then stamped our documents before we entered the country. We didn't mind though, as we collectively agreed that the border stamp would make for a nice souvenir.

Although our passage through Slovenia was short, the roadway was most enjoyable to drive; filled with swerving roads of varying speeds. At one point, we came upon what appeared to be a pig roast on the side of the road. Unable to stop and turn around, the discussion turned to that very topic, pig roasts. A few short kilometers later, we came upon another establishment that was roasting pigs. This time, I was prepared to pull over.

We saw there were three pigs roasting roadside, all on spits, turning in rhythm, synchronized as they slowly turned from upright to stomach up. There were stacks of hickory and apple wood chips piled neatly behind each of the pigs in the sizeable open oven. What a sight and smell for us to enjoy, although we departed without a purchase.

Earl kept us on the same highway, and soon, signs for Opatija and Rijeka appeared. It was amazing to me that about 75 minutes ago, we were in Italy, 15 minutes ago we were in Slovenia, and now we were just 10 minutes from our exit in Croatia.

As we took the exit, it was impossible to avoid the sight and vastness of the great Adriatic Sea, a remarkable spectacle. The view gave us great pause; the car fell silent.

The area had a completely different feel than I expected... it seemed as though we were entering a beach resort. Most of the buildings were all painted in light pastel colors, covered in terracotta. Our moods changed as we took the exit.

Earl told us that our destination was on the right, as we pulled up to our hotel. The awaiting parking attendant asked me to pull directly into the parking garage located below the reception desk, and I complied.

As we exited the parking area and crossed the street, we were stunned to learn that the Grand Hotel Cvijeta was situated directly on the Adriatic. From all the pictures I had seen on the internet, it appeared that the hotel was across the street, close to the Adriatic, but not literally on it!

We were in Venice, a few days before we arrived in Croatia, I felt the heels of my feet beginning to crack. The cracking could have been due to the intense heat over the past few days, or just a result of my dry skin. I did my best to ignore the ensuing pain.

Grin and bear it, Jim!

Unfortunately, by the time we arrived in Croatia, my right heel had split so deeply it had begun to bleed. The fracture in my skin was so deep that I couldn't control the blood flow. I went to the local pharmacy just up the street and purchased some Neosporin and Band-Aids, in hopes that it would allow me to continue uninterrupted with our travels.

After the ride from Venice, stopover, and walk in Trieste, a short stay in Slovenia, and arrival in Croatia, I may have exasperated my situation to the point of no return. Now, both of my heels were in horrible condition. I am not one to moan but had to admit that I was suffering. I could see the gaping split running from the top of my heel to nearly the bottom of my foot. The gash appeared to be hazardous; it was so significant.

In Croatia, we followed our usual routine, which involves walking around and discovering our surroundings. This day was like all the others; we walked in and out of shops with an occasional pause for a refreshing cocktail. Several hours into our walk, I reached my absolute threshold of pain and found that I couldn't take another step. By the time this realization set in, we were miles from our hotel.

Due to my condition, I felt utterly helpless, if not completely stranded. I knew that we would have to call a taxi to rescue us, well, to save me. We popped into the nearest hotel and did what was necessary and called for help. Within 10 minutes, we were on our way back to our hotel.

Finally, back at the hotel, I went to our room, turned on the hot water in the bathtub, and soaked my split, bloody feet. A good, long soaking, followed by a generous application of Neosporin and bandages seemed like the perfect solution. Once the ointment was applied, I put a pair of socks on my feet to help keep the bandages in place, offering me relief. Now with covered, medicated feet, I went to bed.

The following morning, I removed the Band-Aids and applied more Neosporin to my wounds. Much to my dismay, I noticed that not only was the cut on my right heel deeper, but my left heel had also divided more extensively as well.

Dressing both wounds with more Neosporin, Band-Aids, and socks, I carefully placed my feet into my sandals. Putting the strap on my heels took the most imaginable concentration and Zen moment of my life! I was in real pain.

We went down to the parking garage to retrieve our car and began the journey to our next adventure. We drove on the Nova Cesta, also known as Route 66, we headed south on our quest. As we were driving down the curving road of Route 66, I found myself needing to use the clutch a great deal to help compensate for the up and down curviness of our passageway.

Since my heels needed to be on the floor of the car to operate the clutch and gas pedal safely, the more I pressed the clutch, the more pain I experienced.

I never realized how much my feet moved during a regular drive in a manual shift car.

Seemingly out of nowhere, I reached my brink of pain. I couldn't bear it another minute. Sasha and I began looking for a bright green cross, which signifies a pharmacy. We passed many of these green signs, but none of the lights were lit, meaning they were closed for business. I quickly realized the reason for this: today was Sunday, a day of rest.

My fear grew, as I came to the realization that we needed to find a hospital. I have traveled through Europe many times with various groups of musicians, who have been in need of medical assistance, so I was accustomed to helping those in need. This time, however, I was the one who needed the help.

Out of desperation, I decided to turn around and head in a different direction. I turned the car around and headed north. Before I knew it, we entered a gated area. "No!" I panicked. "Where the heck are we?"

I took a slip of paper out of the waiting timed machine and passed through the gate. It read "Free of charge for the first 15 minutes."

Okay, so it is not going to take me 15 minutes to find a place to turn around and leave, right? We made our way down the road looking for a place to turn around, when my beautiful wife yelled the words, "There is a hospital just ahead of us!"

I pulled over immediately. As I jumped out of the car, Daniel followed, as he informed me that he needed to go use the bathroom. I hobbled into the building as fast as I could. As we passed from room to room, I could have mistaken the hospital for a swanky, upscale hotel.

Although my feet were a mess, my youngest needed to use the facilities and it was my duty to assist him. Luckily, Daniel spotted the restroom at the same time I saw the reception desk. I approached the receptionist and asked where I can find the attending physician. They told me I had passed by the room on my way to the reception desk. Although I was eager to turn back and discover the doctor's office, I waited for Daniel to finish doing his duty. The receptionist continued, "You came at a good time, the doctor is here until 16:00." It was now 15:20. Fate was apparently on my side.

Once Daniel was back, we both headed toward the examination room we initially passed during our walkthrough of the building. I knocked on the door and heard a voice from behind saying, "Please come in." I entered the room, blinded by happiness, as I felt I was about to get some real care for my split, burning heels.

The doctor spoke perfect English, despite the fact that we were in a foreign country. Elated, I signaled to Daniel to get Sasha and Phillip, who were back in the car waiting for us, as I wanted them to knew what was happening. They arrived at the room just as I was explaining the state of my heels to the doctor. After my explanation, she had me sit on the examination table for a closer look.

Within 5 minutes, she had my feet covered with disinfectant lotion, creams, soothing medications, and a heavenly wrap of soft cushiony gauze. I, —well my feet— were so relieved, as the pain was now fading into a sea of medication.

I couldn't find the words to thank the nurse for her kind assistance. I believe I must have thanked her ten times over and in many different phrases. I explained how much better I felt, all due to her help. She shared her a heartfelt smile and offered me her good wishes.

She wrote a medical prescription for a cleanser, antibiotic cream, and a skin softener to get my heels back into working order. She also included more dressing to cover my heels with, after applying the medicated creams.

The attending physician suggested strongly, that when we got home, I set up a pedicure appointment as soon as possible. I promised her, and my wife, that I would. For the record, as of writing this today on September 18th, I have already had my first pedicure and will schedule another around October 1st.

The doctor asked me for my driver's license and passport, so she could write a proper prescription. She needed my name and date of birth to make the prescription official. Once we filled out all the necessary paperwork, she handed me the bill.

Unbelievably, the invoice was for a staggering 80 Kuna or the equivalent of $10 US dollars. I happily paid and thanked her again for her kindness and welcome attention.

As we walked back to the car, I noticed one fantastic thing: I could walk without any pain. I knew she just wrapped up my feet, but I tell you honestly, it felt like a miracle. I spent the remainder of the day without any discomfort.

The next day, we walked into the pharmacy and filled the prescriptions. The total cost of the antibiotics and healing creams was about $40 US dollars. That price made me stop and think that many, if not all, homeopathic items are readily available and suggested by the pharmacy. It doesn't seem that the bureaucracy of rising health care costs has affected Croatia, or most of Europe, offering food for thought.

I was able to enjoy the remainder of our days in Croatia, and beyond, after just a few applications of the prescribed medication. What a relief. Hvala Hrvatskoj — thank you, Croatia!

Minor Miracle

"Don't believe in miracles - depend on them." ~Laurence J. Peter

Journal Entry: October 28, 2016

When booking an orchestra, one of the things I must take into consideration is the minimum number of strings required at each performance. When I receive instructions that state the string count is 14/12/9/8/6, that translates to 14 first violins, 12-second violins, nine viola, eight cello, and six basses.

On this particular day, we had a run-out performance to Richardson Auditorium in Princeton, New Jersey. The performance was set to begin at 8 p.m., which meant the provided symphony buses would pick up the musicians starting at 5:30 p.m.

Our newly appointed music director would be at the helm of the production, leading the orchestra's performance. We were performing an all Tchaikovsky program, which included his exciting 5th Symphony. When Tchaikovsky writes a symphony, it always requires a careful balance of musicians in the string section.

Under normal conditions, if a member of our orchestra is feeling ill, I usually receive a call well before 3 p.m. A call at or before that hour usually allows me enough time to engage a substitute player, who can subsequently catch the bus, and make it to the performance without too much stress.

Obviously, the later someone calls in sick, the less time I have to find a suitable replacement. In cases of last-minute hiring, I have a list of players who live near each of our run-out venues. I created this file so that the organization would be better protected in these situations. Because I am prepared to replace a sick player at a moment's notice, I feel better protected in my own position as well. Beyond protecting the organization and myself, comes the most important aspect: protecting the artistic product. After all, that is what people are paying money to see and hear.

Just before leaving my home office, I print out the seating roster for the evening's performance. I place three copies into my bag, as I head to my car. One copy goes on the musicians' bulletin board, and the others are placed stage right and left.

Now, heading towards the New Jersey Turnpike, driving east on Route 280. By this time, I am confident that the musicians who were on the roster, will remain on the list.

Some years earlier, when we were performing in Princeton, I encountered the following situation. The dress rehearsal finished at 6 p.m. (for an 8 p.m. performance) when our principal harpist took ill. When I say, "ill" I don't mean the run-of-the-mill cold or flu— I mean, so sick, that there was no way they could physically perform two hours later.

If a string player does get sick at the 11th hour, I may suck it up and not replace them, as there is strength in numbers. However, in cases when you have only one harpist, we consider them a soloist, because no one else is playing their part, I need to find a substitute. On this particular program, we were performing the Bruch Scottish Fantasy. This work relies heavily on the soloistic qualities of the harpist, their ability to follow the conductor, all the while accompanying the violin soloist. It's a tall order.

We have a performance in less than two hours, and we are 75 minutes away from New York City. Bringing in one of my top players from the city is not an option, with the time constraint. However, I know two harpists who live just 15-or -so minutes from Richardson Hall, who are perfectly capable of playing on a very high level.

I called them in-proximity order. The first candidate answered, but informed me they were in San Juan, playing with the symphony all week. Strike one! Nearly ready to panic, I called candidate number two. One ring, two rings, three, finally, I heard a "Hello?" on the other end.

I explained my situation to the harpist. They began to respond, and it didn't sound promising. While listening to learn of their availability, my mind was already thinking about substituting the harp with a synthesizer player. Perhaps they can cover the harp part on their instrument. My mind was racing. The harpist continued, "I just got home from a nice dinner with friends and was about to pour a glass of wine. I will hold off on the wine and come to Richardson to cover the performance."

Can you imagine the relief I felt? Problem solved, and no one was any the wiser of the trauma I had endured in finding a solution. This level of desperation was something I had never experienced before, well, at least not on that level.

Back to today, I am cruising just above the speed limit on the New Jersey Turnpike, when my phone rings. The first thing I noticed was that it was 6:22 p.m. and I immediately assumed it was too late for a sick call, so it must be a routine call, right?

Wrong!

It was our associate principal bass calling to inform me that they had missed the provided bus transportation and that they were not going to be able to make the performance.

"WHAT?!" I was furious. "Are you serious, pulling out at this ridiculous hour? How am I supposed to fill your chair in less than two hours?!"

After sharing more unpleasantries with my player, I knew that there was nothing I could do about it, but needed to dig into my bag of tricks and work a miracle.

There have been times during my career when I thought, "Well, they finally got me." for some reason, I didn't feel defeated and thought I could still fill the chair.

I knew that there was at least one competent bassist (on my radar) who lived just minutes away from Richardson Hall. Of course, I decided to call him first. I did, but with no luck, as I was sent to voicemail.

I had another bassist on my list, who lived just north of Princeton. I dialed his number, mind racing, thoughts uncertain, and partial panic beginning to settle in. While the phone was ringing, I had time to assess my possible failure.

Dan answered. I stated that I was in a difficult position, but would be grateful if he could cover the concert, which at this point, was just one hour away. Dan told me he had just finished a rehearsal in Philadelphia and was heading home. I knew he had to pass Princeton on his way home, so I began to think that this might work. Without missing a beat, I asked "When do you think you could be in the Princeton area? "According to my GPS, 20 minutes," he told me.

It is at times like this that I feel I should play the lottery more often. A perfect storm, resolved by circumstance.

"Hey, Jim," Dan continued, "The only problem is that I do not have any concert clothes with me." He was referring to his tuxedo. I told him that we traveled with a wardrobe trunk and that we had about a dozen suits and tuxedos in the trunk. When Neeme Järvi left the organization, he donated many of his suits and tuxedos to us. An excellent conductor, musician, and man, one who I truly missed when he moved on.

I briefed our very competent stagehands on the turn of events and asked them to prepare several tuxedos for Dan to choose. At 7:40, Dan arrived, and by 7:48 he was suited up. Dan was ready to join the section and at 8:00 p.m., the show began.

I was the hero of the night, and everyone was talking about the miracle I managed to pull off. The truth is, I just made the call that happened to work, a stroke of luck you may say? Genius by some, a duty from others; I accept both assessments.

What most don't know is that the whole ordeal caused me a great deal of anxiety. I felt the need to produce, the need to fill out the section. All par for the job, which most take for granted, including management. It is at times like these that it becomes very apparent to me that most, if not all of the members of the orchestra management, have no real idea what I do, nor the toll it takes on me to get the job done.

When the concert was over, and r the hour drive home complete, I took my tuxedo off for the night. I then poured myself a glass of Pinot Grigio, cut a hunk of Torino cheese into bite-sized pieces, sliced two small tomatoes, and put my feet up on the waiting ottoman, with a job well done.

Rijeka

"You haven't really been anywhere until you've got back home."
~Terry Pratchett

August 17 Day 10, 14 kilometers

As we pulled into Rijeka, I see immediately why my friend and colleague told me not to stay here, but instead in Opatija. Rijeka is a vast industrial city, which the surroundings which indicate. Although we didn't stay in this city, I am glad we visited.

Rijeka is the principal seaport, which sits on the Kvarner Bay, an inlet of the Adriatic Sea. It's the third largest city in Croatia, after Zagreb and Split. Historically, because of its strategic position and its excellent deep-water Port, the city was fiercely contested especially amongst Italy, Hungary, and Croatia, it has changed hands and demographics many times over the course of centuries.

Roman Arch

The ancient wall that is behind the Church of St. Sebastian is closely connected to a monument known as the "Roman Arch" or "Gate." After doing some research on this visually compelling architecture, I learned that Old Gate is the oldest monument in Rijeka. Dating from 1700, the Gate has been the focus of many historians who have studied this land. In the 19ᵗʰ century, it was first considered to be a triumphal arch, erected in honor of Emperor Claudius. However, a Rijeka historian proved it to be the gate of the fortress. Yet another archeologist pointed out that the entrance of the city (The Gate of Tarsatika) is the only ornament remaining on the monument facing the sea.

We visited the Gradski Toranj (City Tower), the incredibly interesting third-century remains of the ancient Principia at Tarsatica, as well as Korzo, Rijeka super promenade. Afterward, we enjoyed a nice walk along Užarska Street (which is one of the main thoroughfares in the city), which boasted any and everything you can imagine.

At the end of Užarska Street is the Church of Saint Mary of the Assumption. The church is a highly attractive medieval building, which is a must-see" when visiting Rijeka.

After spending a beautiful day seeing these exciting sights, it was time to return to our hotel. Before leaving, we needed to pay the tariff on the meter where we had parked for the day. We entered the ticket into the awaiting slot, to learn the amount of our stay. We quickly learned the payment machine did not accept Euros. My darling wife to the rescue volunteered to convert some Euros into the local currency of the Kuna.

Once we paid the parking charge, Sasha realized that she had converted a bit more money than we needed for the parking bill. Of course, we now needed to spend the extra Kuna before leaving the city, as we were set to depart for Austria in the morning.

We spotted a tiny bakery, just outside of the parking facility. We jumped out of the car and darted to the open takeout window, just in front of our car. We had enough for a half dozen Kroštule, which are lightly powdered fried dough fingers, served with a side of raspberry jam. We all agreed that we had never, ever, tasted anything quite like it before at home or during our travels. An error transformed into a delicacy, indeed.

Just Do It

"If you want to conquer fear, don't sit home and think about it. Go out and get busy." ~Dale Carnegie

Journal entry: February 2, 2017, 12:28 a.m.

Mentally, I am beyond exhausted, as my responsibilities over the past few weeks reached an overwhelming peak. As much as I love working, I am not sure I can take on one more project, one more thought, one more detail, or one more anything.

I decided to compartmentalize the various projects and think of each as a separate entity. I need to balance the six ongoing projects I'm working on, as well as my position at the Symphony. My life at the Symphony almost runs on autopilot, except for last minute sick calls or other emergencies, since I have so many years of experience under my belt.

However, looming was the Games of Thrones Tour, Zelda Tour, Final Fantasy Tour, New York City Fashion show with Michael Kors, along with finalizing my Carnegie Hall series. Oh, I nearly forgot, the Irish Tenors! This all makes for a full schedule in the days and weeks to come.

A few weeks ago, I was approached by a Chicago-based company to work up a price quote for a multi-city tour of the HBO mega-hit, Games of Thrones. I am not much of a TV watcher, so I am not aware of the exposure of the show Games of Thrones until I conduct a Google search.

As soon as I finished reading the email invitation, I found the name and phone number of the person who sent me the proposal, Fritz, and picked up the phone and called him. He answered the phone by saying, "That was fast!"

After a few words of small talk, I asked Fritz the million-dollar question, "How did you hear about me?"

He replied that he and Giovanni from GBP work together and he learned of my abilities through him.

On our call, I gained a good understanding of the production needs, (meaning the orchestra size as well as any backline items required (percussion rental, chorus enhancement, etc.). This particular tour required a three-city budget, for New York, Philadelphia, and Washington D.C. The same orchestra of 33 musicians will rehearse and perform in all three venues and magically get from location to location as if sprinkled with pixie dust.

How do I put this multi-city tour together? Where shall the tour originate that would be the most cost-effective? After consideration of the multiple possibilities, my thoughts began to solidify. I decided to hire a New York-based orchestra to travel to Philadelphia and Washington D.C., as the final performance was at Madison Square Garden in New York City.

The budget is shaping up, but before I can finalize the cost, I need a bit more information. Pressing questions running through my head: "Am I responsible for renting a rehearsal studio in New York?"

"What are the conductor's needs, when is s/he available?"

"What time will we schedule the rehearsal?"

After emailing Fritz, I learned the rehearsal conductor for all three shows, lived in Boston. I asked him to find out if the conductor could make a noon rehearsal on Saturday, February 25 in New York City. A few hours later, I learned the conductor could indeed make that rehearsal date. With this final piece of information, I could nail down the cost to rent a well-known rehearsal studio in midtown Manhattan.

The day after the first rehearsal, we would have a 3 p.m. rehearsal and 8 p.m. performance at the Wells Fargo Arena in downtown Philadelphia. Game of Thrones composer, Ramin Djawadi is also the conductor for the complete series of concerts.

Because we have two run-outs at a considerable distance, I decided to see how much it would cost to charter a bus. My thinking was simple; it would likely be easier to secure an orchestra if I was able to provide transportation to the other performances. The second advantage of this plan? The musicians would all travel together, ensuring their timely, and collective arrival at all venues.

After Googling *"Bus charter,"* I began gathering costs for the tour. I have to consider if a bus could the bus fit three string basses, five cellos, along with 33 passengers?

I called a bass playing buddy of mine, to gain his input on my proposed idea. He told me it was a very reasonable request to place the instruments in the seats on the coach. He also told me that one bass would take up two seats. Therefore, I would need six seats to accommodate three basses. He also told me that each cello would take up one seat and the owner of the cello would sit next to their instrument in the adjacent seat. That was 11 seats dedicated to instruments and 33 for passengers. That total is 44, I priced out a 55-passenger bus for each trip, so people would have additional room to spread out.

The company I ultimately chose, provided high back reclining seats, a restroom, CD and DVD players with drop down TV's, AM-FM Stereo, heat, and air conditioning. All the amenities would add to the comfort of the charter. I included the cost to the bottom line of the overall budget. I feel it is money well spent!

Concurrently, while dealing with the bus rental, I had emails out to the Pennsylvania and D.C. local musicians' unions as well as to the Federation touring department in New York City requesting various rules, pay scales, and touring information. Within a few hours of discussion with the Federation, we mutually agreed that we would use the New York rate for the Madison Square Garden date and the higher of the two scales for both runout venues, that being, the Washington D.C. rates

I contacted the D.C. and Pennsylvania musician's unions to request their pay scale rates. Once obtained, I was able to produce a complete budget for my new Chicago client.

It was time to begin finalizing the budget: to do so, I plugged in the numbers of the salaries, pension, work dues, over scale for principals, and for the New York date, a health and welfare benefit. Beyond that, I added in the payroll tax percentage, bus charters, rehearsal studio rental, and finally, my fee.

Even with adding in the two bus charters, my quote came in nearly twenty thousand dollars less than my closest competitor, and as a result, I won the bid.

I secured all 33 musicians within a 48-hour period. I attribute half of my hiring to be due to luck and the other half to those who want to perform in venues that have a capacity of 18,000-plus.

Looking at my schedule, I saw that on, the day of the Pennsylvania sound check and performance, I have a concert in Morristown, New Jersey with the Symphony. The two locations are about 90 miles apart from each other. My 3 p.m. performance in Morristown should conclude by 5 p.m. and the performance in Pennsylvania is set to begin at 8 p.m.

However, I realize there is a 5 p.m. sound check in Pennsylvania that I must attend! Easy fix, I will line up one of my musicians to oversee the start and stop of the sound check and will assume my regular responsibilities for the performance once I arrive.

On the day of the performance by 5:10 p.m., I was in my car heading south on route 202 to Pennsylvania. Quite unexpectedly, I hit absolutely no traffic and enjoyed smooth sailing from door to door. I pulled into my designated parking spot at the Pennsylvania arena, earlier than expected. When I took my iPhone off the windshield mount, I noted the time: it was just 6:46 p.m.

I entered the building, passed through security, and found the dressing rooms where the orchestra was taking their break. I asked my point person if the sound check ran smoothly and she confirmed that all went as planned.

A few minutes later, a gentleman named Jerome introduced himself as the Game of Thrones tour manager. I soon learned just how capable Jerome was and how organized he had all matters in place. He greeted me and offered to take me to the dining area, so I could grab a bite to eat as well as a much-needed cup of coffee.

As part of the tour package, I arranged a hot buffet between the sound check and performances at all venues. The touring company agreed as they knew it would be nearly impossible to have the musicians leave the arena and find a meal, in between the sound check and performance.

The show began at precisely 8:05 p.m. and the orchestra performed to a sold-out house. At exactly 10:25 p.m., the show concluded to a round of thunderous applause. I witnessed the monumental success before my eyes, a far cry from the non-profit work I have experienced during my entire career.

I was not only in awe of their production team but also how efficiently my day worked. I observed and digested the massive differences between a non-profit and profit organizational approach and the giant financial backing both. I logged the event into my memory, and later, in my trusty journal.

By 10:45 p.m. I was back in my car heading north on the Pennsylvania Turnpike. Shortly after midnight, I pulled into the driveway of our East Hanover home, thinking about that glass of chilled Pinot Grigio that was awaiting me in the refrigerator.

"All the world's indeed a stage
And we are merely players
Performers and portrayers
Each another's audience
Outside the gilded cage" ~Peart

Project 2 and 3: The Legend of Zelda and ongoing Final Fantasy tours. By this time, I have presented over 39 budgets for these performances, which I gathered from my North American contractors. My people have done their homework on the cost of a 56-piece orchestra, union fees, percussion rental, and price for securing a 20-member chorus in their respective cities.

Once the fall Zelda schedule is in place, I will need to reconnect with my team of contractors to have them send agreements, binding them to the production and GBP Live. I oversee all contracts and assist in the negotiations of all fees. I carefully check each spreadsheet, to relieve the anxiety that the contractor made any errors, forced or otherwise, in the budget. Being a fellow contractor for decades, I knew all the ins and outs of the budget, including where and how to bury some fees into the full budget. Thus, I know exactly where to look.

As the tour date announcement draws nearer, I find myself spending more time coordinating multi-city options, such as using one orchestra to play in Cleveland and Columbus, Kansas City and Des Moines, Norfolk and Durham, Edmonton and Calgary, and so forth. The benefit of using the same group in two cities is that there would be no need for a full rehearsal at the second venue, only a soundcheck which saves the company money.

The Distant Worlds, Music from Final Fantasy tour has proven to be less of a challenge to put together. Working similarly, I have solicited numerous contractors in various cities for a price quote on the show. Most came back with a reasonable quote which I still scrutinized but ultimately accepted. I am in the process of gathering final contracts from both Zelda and Final Fantasy and getting them executed by my superiors.

Preparing my master calendar, I entered all rehearsal and performance dates, as well as calendar reminders to get backstage security lists from all contractors two weeks before their show. I also set reminders to line up payment schedules from each of the venues to the contractors. All of these tour aspects were on my shoulders, all part of my new responsibilities as a music coordinator for North America.

Project 4: Michael Kors Fashion Show in New York City, Michelin Tires, and *NIKE*!

Happily, I am reunited with my Parisian clients and friends to engage the musicians needed for the February 14th and 15th fashion show in New York City. Having worked with Ivan and Thomas on the *NIKE* experience last year, I was curious to see what they had in store for me this time.

The *NIKE* experience was indeed one of those once in a lifetime gigs. We were hired to perform the music written for the unveiling of the summer Olympic uniforms in Brazil. I had to hire a 40-piece orchestra to play music with the composer and keyboardist, Thomas Prequel.

Before getting into the Fashion Show with Michael Kors, Ivan and I were in discussions over a set of dates. Michelin Tires, another multibillion-dollar company, had sponsored a set of performances to take place in the middle of the Palm Springs desert.

We were to supply musicians for one rehearsal and five 30-minute performances for the invited friends of the giant company, Michelin. One small complication: all six services were spread out over 11 days. Because the dates were spread out over a nearly two-week period, as well as the location of the work, finding musicians who are available for all the dates could be challenging.

In fact, the Michelin job was my first desert gig, ever. I considered that due to this location, I needed to remedy the heat and shelter possibilities.

I learned that Ivan was already on top of this issue, as well as many others. There were many companies involved in the Michelin event, from tent rentals, stage builders, bar and recreation centers, lighting crews, and special effects, all who would play a part in the event.

In that neck of the woods, I secured my number one contractor, Al Metz, to manage my work. After a lot of back and forth with Ivan and Al, we came to our final agreement. The details of the Palm Springs gig were nailed down, and I could take a back seat while Al ran the show. Al handled all of the on-site preparations, including hiring of the musicians. Consequently, I had personally earned another paycheck with minimal effort.

I received the call from my French connection, Ivan, with this subject line: *NIKE* needs musicians!

On Mon, Feb 22, 2016, at 6:40 p.m., Ivan wrote:

Hi, Jim!
So, here's a full recap. The orchestra will play with Prequel, as well as the music of Prequel, that you can listen here: https://soundcloud.com/prequell (probably some new tracks, not the one from Soundcloud but you have the spirit).
Firstly, here's a breakdown of the orchestra that we need:

Musicians A:

- 8 1st Violins
- 7 2nd Violin
- 6 Violas

- 4 Celli
- 1 contrabass
- 4 percussionists

Musicians B:

- 8 brass players
- 8 percussionists.

There's going to be two performances of around 30 minutes each, on March 17th. If we manage to have them both in a two and a half hour span, we don't have to pay more, right? I asked for rates of both possibilities? So far, it appeared that the first performance will be at 2:30 p.m., and the second at around 4 p.m.

Regarding the rehearsals, there are two options: the first option is to do two rehearsals that are each two and a half hours on March 15th (how long do the musicians need a break between each?) and one rehearsal of 2 ½ hours on March 17th and the two performances of 30 minutes on March 17th The second option is to hold on 2 ½ hour rehearsal on March 15th, another rehearsal of two and a half hours on March 17th, and the two performances of 30 minutes on March 17th.

The rehearsals and the event will take place at the Moynihan Station in New York City. I need to have the rates be inclusive of *every* cost, and if there are costs on top, please specify details. I'm open to ideas to save costs, feel free to propose!

Also, here's our concept for the live performance: the idea is to have the orchestra set up in a series of circles. The first and the largest circle would be composed of strings, the second, with the percussionists, and have Thomas/Prequel (the artist) in the middle solo, with keyboards.

We will be using on-ear monitors for everyone: the click and the tracks will be played from Thomas' computer to the in-ear pieces worn by the musicians. Are you comfortable with that?

Let me know if you need anything else from me. As soon as I have this information, I will be able to discuss this with our clients and give you a firm answer.

Many thanks,
Ivan

I was able to answer Ivan's email thoroughly, within just a few hours. With the event being only 21 days away, I needed to get moving. More pressure to work with this tight deadline.

An hour after sharing the budget with Ivan, and finalizing the rehearsal and performance schedule, he inquired about a possible live broadcast or streaming option. I needed to price out how much it would cost to videotape the performance. All recordings carry different rules and rates, and I felt the need to learn that information from our local union and the Federation, before giving an answer.

Sent: Thursday, March 10, 2016, 5:17 p.m.
Subject: possible videotape?

Greetings all,
Under the Single Engagement, Classical Wage Scale, governed by The Local; I have booked 47 musicians to perform two rehearsals and one 30-minute performance. The work is set to take place on March 15th and 17th at Moynihan Station (360 West 33rd Street, between 8th and 9th Avenues). Gemini Music Production LTD is handling the payroll for the event. The event itself is to perform the Music of Thomas Prequel. All union fees (health, pension, etc.) have been approved by the producers and Gemini has sent them an invoice.

Today, I have been approached by the producers to see what the cost would be to videotape the 30-minute performance, which would be used by all or part of the production for publicity purposes. The video would be used on their website, as well as posted on social media (Facebook, Twitter, etc.).

In addition, I have also learned that this performance is part of the unveiling of uniforms for the upcoming 2016 summer Olympics in Brazil by *NIKE*.

My questions:

What other funds are needed for the video and usage?

Do we need to file a "B" form? If not, please let me know which form is required?

Before we can move forward, I need to produce a budget. Once this happens, I will learn if the videotaping will be possible.

I apologize for the urgency of this request, but I only learned about this option an hour ago.

Thank you.

The Union, Federation, Ivan, and I shared a few dozen emails before finalizing the written contract. Once the agreement was signed, I was able to begin the next stage of the process, which was securing the musicians.

After obtaining everything I needed from the Federation, I was armed with a complete budget to share with both Ivan and the production company.

We were off to the races! Things are heading in the right direction. The inertia of the event began to swing firmly to the positive. That energy morphed throughout the event, and before we knew it, we realized we had a giant hit on our hands. The success of the production felt as large as the company itself!

After the performance concluded, thanked Ivan and Thomas for having me play a part in the process. I knew they were both heading back to Paris that evening and didn't wish to take up too much of their time, so I made my exit. When I returned to my office, I sent an email of thanks.

Dear Ivan and Thomas,

I want to thank you both for trusting me with your musical needs for the *NIKE* project. The musicians and I enjoyed ourselves thoroughly. I hope to work with you again sometime soon.

Continued success,

Merci beaucoup!

Thomas "Prequal" Roussel wrote back:
Sent: Monday, March 21, 2016, at 9:44 a.m.

Hello, Jim!
Thank you so much for your energy, your efficiency, and your professionalism! Say hello and thanks to the musicians for me. Too bad we didn't take a picture altogether.
I'm sure we'll work again soon together.

Cheers from Paris!

Sent: Le 21 mars 2016 à 15:12, Ivan Striga a écrit:
Hi Jim, Sorry for the late reply, we've been back in Paris since yesterday morning and our last days in NYC were quite packed!

THANK YOU and all the musicians for your 100% commitment to this project, which was quite a challenge, as well as your ability to deal with our last-minute requirements. You will definitely be our first point of contact for any future live music projects in the New York area - which I hope we do! It was an absolute pleasure to work with you.

Ivan
I replied with enthusiasm,

It was *my* great pleasure to work with you and Ivan. We enjoyed ourselves very much. I hope to work with you in the future on any musical project. We need to work together again so we can take a proper photograph!

Sincères remerciements pour votre gentillesse (with fond memories).

The New York Fashion Week show required 20 string players, but there was a caveat, which made the job of obtaining musicians a significant challenge.

I learned that each of the musicians needed to fit, or shall I say look, the part to the fashion show attendees. Generally speaking, men and women between the ages of 25-40, handsome, pretty, tall, and thin. Under any other circumstance, I could be accused by some of the discriminatory actions if I did not employ my "regulars." However, those were the requirements that came with the job, and I accepted knowing the massive task at hand. Meeting the needs of the fashion show added multiple hours to the task which ate into other pressing matters waiting for me on my desk.

I documented that to hire the 20 needed musicians, I would need to submit over 67 possibilities. Each email to my client included a photograph of each musician that I obtained via Facebook or another internet source. In the end, I hired some tall women, African American women, all with sharp distinguished facial features men who had beards, as well as rugged facial features; they were in high demand. It was an incredibly tedious process, slow in the making, but in retrospect, I understand the needs of the production as a whole.

Once all the musicians were secured, I was asked to set up a clothing fitting with the Michael Kors office in Manhattan. Not an enormous task, but another time-consuming chore that must get done immediately. Each musician was going to receive a complete Michael Kors outfit, from head to toe. Measurements of each musician needed to take place so the production can provide them with a custom set of Kors clothes as well as his stylish shoes.

These days, it seems everyone that I am working with would like things to happen yesterday! They expect answers to questions before they have even asked them, it seems. I am not complaining, just observing.

For the Kors show, I needed to configure the rehearsal times and location with Ivan. Ultimately, we agreed that the full orchestra rehearsal would take place from 7-10 p.m. at Spring Studios in New York City, just south of the Holland Tunnel. We will use the same location for the following morning's live production.

I gave the musicians a 7 a.m. call time for the following day, even though the actual performance wasn't set to take place before 10 a.m. The musicians were hired to play a 12-minute work with composer Thomas Roussel, otherwise known as Prequel. Although we were set to arrive very early, and possibly not be needed for hours, I figured this would allow the necessary time for any final fittings, necessary adjustments, and makeup application.

In addition to all the aforementioned planning details, I needed to produce a precise budget. This needed to include a price for "live streaming," so we could enable people from all around the world to watch the show as it was happening, live! That aspect of the budget is something that I have not produced in my professional career. No problem though, I will just make a call to the west coast American Federation of Musician's office and learn the numbers I need.

It may all sound simple, but nothing is simple when dealing with the Federation. I don't say this because the Federation folks are difficult to work with, on the contrary. The Federation staff is extremely thorough in their work and in the questions, they have for me regarding my various projects. Because of the complexity of this particular project, that being "Live streaming," we were dealing with new and somewhat uncharted territory.

Only after having a long, detailed conversation about how I thought the Kors event was going to unfold were we able to come up with the verbiage, as well as the actual fees required for the musicians. With the final numbers in hand, I can insert them into the growing budget.

After all these years, calculating a budget has become routine. In fact, I have created ready-made templates for nearly every musical scenario.

There was only one loose end that needed resolution, which is regarding, who will own the intellectual property (the footage of the orchestra and the recording it produces) of the live shoot? The owner becomes the signatory to the contract with the Federation. The signatory becomes responsible for every aspect of recording and videotape.

Whoever signs the contract, becoming the signatory, is responsible for paying the same initial fee every six months, if the recording and or video remains accessible via social media or on any website, including but not limited to, YouTube. I knew one thing for certain: I was not going to be the signatory to this agreement.

Still, on my checklist, I need to inform my payroll company of the new projects, provide payrolls, invoices, confirm dates, descriptions, and my favorite part, document the events in my journal. I accomplished my task by taking each detail a little at a time. I began sending emails of information to the musicians, the union, and payroll company, one by one.

Going back to the performance schedule, I imagine Ivan, Thomas, and I would have a drink after the 10 p.m. rehearsal. I began to think about how little time I would have at home, back in New Jersey, before leaving the house for our 7 a.m. call time the following morning.

It takes about 35 minutes without traffic to get from our home to the Spring Studio. Although it doesn't take an hour and a half for the trip, I know my personal comfort zone of arrival time. To me, "on time" means showing up before everyone else. I know I will need to leave home no later than 5:30 a.m. to make it to the New York, location without issue.

By now, my body and mind are approaching exhaustion. I thought about having a bite to eat or drink with Ivan and Thomas. If we spend a short time together, it will be at least midnight before I retrieve my car from the valet. I wouldn't arrive home before 1 a.m. Losing that much sleep is unacceptable under these circumstances.

I came up with the perfect remedy: staying in New York after the evening rehearsal, rather than commuting back to New Jersey. I searched for the closest hotel in proximity to the studio. The Hilton Garden Inn Tribeca was just 190 feet from the venue, door to door. With little thought, I booked a room and felt an inner peace knowing that the travel portion of this production was no longer a variable. Score one for the contractor!

While entering the address of the hotel location into my agenda, I inadvertently noticed that my Carnegie Hall series was starting *this* coming Saturday, this must be a joke, right? As alarmed as I was, I didn't jump out of my skin, because I knew that I had secured the personnel for all services some months ago. However, I did need to prepare an email reminder of the date and times for the hired musicians. More details, more brain power, more responsibility; the thought of the hotel stay was becoming more and more comforting! I banged out the Carnegie reminder pretty quickly but realized I needed to collect more payroll information for the series. More emails, more bookkeeping, and more brain power. Press on Jim, press on.

While juggling all of these events, my phone was ringing off the hook. One of those calls was from my colleague at the Symphony, inquiring about payroll for the 92 musicians who worked during the last pay period.

I dropped everything, or shall I say, I stacked all other projects in order of priority to the right of my computer keyboard. Producing the payroll took under an hour, but the energy required bore its weight on my already taxed brain. I am now feeling the full effects of exhaustion but somehow, am able to function at a reasonably high level. This has been one of my strongest assets in the working world. In these, my later years, I have attributed my success to that very fact; my ability to work, process, function and produce under every possible circumstance.

With the Symphony payroll complete, I began focusing on the Games of Thrones tour. Amidst review of the budget, my phone rang again. This time, it was my colleague from GBP Live on the other end. We were adding more venues to the Zelda tour, and I needed to gather price quotes for Portland, Spokane, Vancouver, and Boston. They also wanted to confirm pricing for Baltimore, Chicago, Nova Scotia, Edmonton, and Calgary. The remaining 30 plus budgets were already in place. I need more time, to deal with more distractions from what I was doing; what was it I was doing, again? Honestly, I can't recall, so Zelda won my focus, for the time being.

Just as I thought there was nothing else I could squeeze into my agenda, an email came through enquiring about a possible booking for a series in

Drexel Hill, Upper Darby, Pennsylvania with the Irish Tenors. The referral came from friend and colleague, Lloyd. Lloyd is the conductor for Celtic Woman, and over the years we have worked together many times with that ensemble. When not working with Celtic Woman, Lloyd conducts the Irish Tenors show, amongst others. It was the touring manager who contacted me via email, at Lloyds request.

We went back and forth on numbers, times, and percussion rental for the Irish Tenors show. I noted a 19-email chain is running back and forth, regarding this possibility. I have witnessed this, time after time; the longer an organization waits to secure an orchestra, the more they feel the pressured into making a decision. Feeling that their back is against the wall, they nearly always lean towards who they know, or as in my case, who recommended me. I am relatively confident I will win the bid.

I feel I am ready to implode. I need to get out of my home office and unwind. Downstairs in our basement apartment, we have an elliptical. The elliptical has been my best friend for years now, great to get my heart pumping, as well as allowing the workout to help keep my mind off what I left behind on my desk. I pressed pause on the computer, tours, and phone, going to a place where I think about nothing but getting my heart rate up and releasing stress.

During my second mile of pumping away, I broke my golden rule and began reflecting on this particular stretch of time in my life, and I realized that the Kors gig, Game of Thrones Tour, Final Fantasy shows, and most of my Symphony obligations are now all up to date. There was a good deal of work yet to accomplish once I hear from GBP Live about the fall Zelda tour. I will need to send all my contractors an email of confirmation, as well as their fully executed contracts. I need to prepare a Dropbox file of all MP3's of the show, as well as PDF's of all the music. I will also send a thorough schedule of the day's events for each city.

Before I knew it, my 45-minute session came to an end. Drenched in sweat, I felt great.

Jim with Michael Kors

Project 5 – The Carnegie Hall series

I have been working as the music contractor for Field Studies, which is a New York-based company that produces musical events, most of which take place at Carnegie Hall. They employ me to hire musicians to enhance various vocal ensembles, during those events.

The schedule for each date in the series is always the same, Saturday rehearsal from 2 p.m. to 3:30 p.m. and then a sound-check at around 6:30 or 7:00 p.m., with a performance commencing at 8:30 p.m. The performances usually run in three sections, that being, they have a beginning, middle, and an end. The ending group is always the featured group, requiring the greatest number of hired musicians to help enrich the overall performance. Save the best for last, as they say.

Over the years, I hire any combination of musicians, from string quartets to a single oboe, flute, to a solo trumpet. But the most common combination that I am asked to secure is a drummer and electric bassist. They are both needed for the rousing gospel number scheduled towards the end of each program. One large item lifted from my duties is the pianist is supplied by Field Studios. What a relief!

On many occasions for the Saturday rehearsal, we will have 2 or 3 groups in various hotels rehearsing for the same Sunday joint culmination. We rehearse in the hotels where the singers are staying with their families. The vocal groups fly in from every city throughout North America and enjoy, for a fee, the chance to perform on the main stage of Carnegie Hall, named Isaac Stern Auditorium. Additionally, the cost of the experience also includes tickets to a Broadway show, all transfers, hotel costs, breakfast, dinner, and airfare.

Over the years, I have had as many as eight performances to book during the complete series of concerts, for any particular set. The series usually runs from mid-February to late April. During this particular year, I have the most shows booked in my career, having a total of 11 series to book and manage. I am happy for the work, but know it will add to my already hectic schedule.

The needs of the day shape up to be something like this: on Saturday in hotel one, we need a violin, cello, and harp. In Hotel two, needed a drummer and bassist, and in hotel three, another drummer and bassist were required. Our total needs translate to a violin, cello, harp, two bassists, and two drummers, who would both be showing up on Sunday for separate sound checks and different performance times.

I usually receive all the musician needs of Field Studies just after Thanksgiving, allowing me plenty of time to secure the best musicians. Because of the odd timing of the Saturday and Sunday schedule, it is rarely problematic for me to fill their needs. Neither the rehearsal nor performance times conflict with Broadway shows, a win for me and the needed musicians.

Even if I am not going to be a performer on one of the series, I will still show up to most of the Saturday rehearsals, but always attend and manage the Sunday sound check and performance.

Once each group is secured, I request the music from Field Studies and begin the arduous task of scanning parts to my players. While looking at the overall schedule, there weren't any incredible problems with this season's line up, but there was an unusually high amount of work get done.

Project 6 – The Irish Tenors

I won the bid! It was not a problematic presentation, but it is still another project thrown into the mix of an already hectic period. Typically, on a basic series like this, I would elect to perform in the percussion section, as well as serve as manager. However, that added another layer of work, concentration, and preparation; time and concentration I did not have.

Still, I was curious. I wanted to perform on the gig but needed more information.

The solution came to me as I sifted through the last email chain. I emailed Lloyd to see if he could send me an advance of the percussion music. Although he was unable to send me the actual music, he did give me a list of instruments that the one percussionist would need to play.

Here is that list of the required instruments: Bass drum, washboard, claves, Field drum, castanets, cabasa, triangle, shakers, cowbell, snare drum, a full set of Chimes, Gong, suspended cymbals, bell tree, spoons, tambourine, xylophone, crash cymbals, mounted tambourine, hi-hat, wind chimes, tom-toms, glockenspiel, finger cymbals, drum set, wood block, and three timpani; enough?

Once I saw the list, I knew I was facing the challenge of not only performing but trying to figure out how I was going to set up the vast number of instruments, logistically. Further, I was to set them up according to the unknown variable, that being, the music itself, which I would not see before the only rehearsal.

My decision to not perform this series became crystal clear. Instead, I hired a versatile percussionist who has a great deal of experience working in the pit of Broadway shows. This would be a walk in the park for him. Done and relieved.

Project 7, life at the Orchestra

Between the New Year and my February 2nd journal entry, the Symphony performed a total of 27 services. We held audition elections, I booked and played with Hip Hop artist, Nelly, I booked the Michael Kors orchestra, and had a working meeting with Giovanni regarding the Zelda/Final Fantasy tours. Additionally, I flew to Palm Springs, California for an 18-hour meeting with the executives in charge of the Michelin event, managed and booked eleven Carnegie Hall events, and did my best to take care of my wife and sons. All this in 33 days. A new record in lunacy in my life!

The past 33 days makes March of 2015 look like a walk in the park. I can't believe I thought of this month as a difficult period. In the chapters to come, you will see the result of my efforts. I can assure you, it does not end pretty, and lessons were learned.

On a lighter note, after my payroll company sent out paychecks for a recent gig, I received the following email:

Sent: Fri, Oct 27, 2017, at 5:18 p.m.
Subject: oh no!

Hi Jim,
I have had a paycheck mishap. Literally, my dog chewed it up when it came through the mail slot today, while I was teaching.

Any chance I can get a replacement? I am so sorry! I can't believe she did this! I have attached a photo…

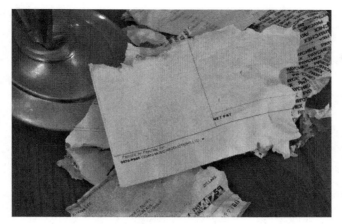

Chewed Check

I replied to my player and included the payroll company:

Sent: Fri, Oct 27, 2017, at 5:43 p.m.
Subject: You are not going to believe this!

If you didn't send the picture, I would have had a harder time buying into your story! But a picture is worth a million bucks ☺
Neil, your thoughts?

Neil responded:
Sent: Fri, Oct 27, 2017, at 6:14 p.m.
Subject: This is a first!

Thanks for the lovely picture. I'll put a replacement check in the mail tomorrow. Normally I would ask you to shred the original but...."

The musician responded: I will keep the dog away from the new check when it arrives and give her the old one to complete the shredding job. So sorry, this won't happen again. I might have to have her teeth removed!

A week later, I was CC'd on the following:
Sent: Fri, Nov 2, 2017, at 2:11 p.m.
Subject: Thank you!

Got the new paycheck and made sure the doggie didn't get to it this time. Thanks again, so sorry for the inconvenience. I really appreciate your help with this situation.

I wrote back to both:

Neil, thanks a million for taking care of the replacement check so quickly! Fran: warning, I may use this story and picture in my next book!

Permission granted: Feel free!

The Culprit

Did I mention that I love my job?

Salzburg

"There are no foreign lands. It is the traveler only who is foreign."
~Robert Louis Stevenson

August 18 Day 11, 400 kilometers

Although Earl told us we needed four hours for our longest leg of the trip, I knew he was not telling the truth. Yes, on the information board I can see it, four hours. However, maps and reality are two entirely different things.

I wish Earl's directions were correct, but this particular trip took us into unchartered territory. In Earl's defense, the roads were incredibly slow, filled with many twists and turns. Each of these forced us to move at a much-reduced speed and speeding up was not a regular option. The entire ride took us an unprecedented 5 hours, and 10 minutes, and yes, I documented it.

As Salzburg came into focus, I do remember from previous trips that the Alps would come alive to our left. Sure enough, a few kilometers later, the Alps came towering over us, a vision worthy of the trip itself.

Along with their grandeur, we were entering the city limits; it was impossible not to see the famed Hohensalzburg Castle which sat high above us to the East, a magnificent sight to behold! Fortunately, there was time and a place to pull over for a brief photo moment.

Our next destination was the Ramada Hotel Salzburg City Center, which was located about 20 minutes from the Castle. From our research, we knew that the hotel was about a 25-minute walk to old town Salzburg. That walking distance may be a bit much for some families, but not for the Neglia's, as we are all avid walkers. I took note that the hotel was just across the street from the train station, in the event we needed to use it for an unexpected journey of exploration.

After our long, somewhat exhausting drive, we checked in to our hotel. Regardless, we rallied together and ventured out, immediately after checking in.

Heading south-east on Südtiroler toward Engelbert-Weiß-Weg, we found ourselves crossing the bridge on the Staatsbrücke. The old town was within reach; I could almost smell the scent of Mozart's home. I hadn't been to Salzburg for more than 20 years, and let me tell you, I was oozing with anticipating to feel her under my feet.

We were heading to the famed Hagenauer House, better known as the home of Mozart, located at Getreidegasse 9. From my preliminary research all those years ago, I had learned that he lived there for twenty-six years of his short 35-year life, from 1747 - 1773.

Once inside of the famed composer's home, I was thoroughly absorbed. I was enjoying watching my family see all that was before them. They saw Mozart's piano, his violins. My particular interest peaked when I looked at letters Mozart wrote to his father and the letters from his father back to our beloved composer. We spent over two hours in Mozart's house, before taking leave and moving on.

Outside, and a little further up on Getreidegasse, I came across a storefront that caught my immediate attention. As I entered a shop, I knew my suspicions were correct, as the shop hosted the holy load of percussion and musical instruments. Oh, happy day! There were the most amazing instruments on display, and all were part of the petting zoo as well as for purchase.

As I walked around the shop, I carefully picked up every instrument in sight, to try them out. I came across a brilliant set of hand-carved wooden whistles, whistles of every animal imaginable. The funny thing is, I had purchased many of these fantastic sounds in Germany some years earlier. All of these instruments and sound effects were still fascinating to me, still holding my attention and desire. I nearly made a purchase knowing that I would just be duplicating my already assumed collection. Talk about being caught up in the moment!

As I turned the corner, I came across an item which peaked my interest higher than almost everything else I sampled. It was a Kalimba, an African musical instrument, that functions as a plucked idiophone or thumb piano.

This thumb piano didn't have a specific resonating chamber; this entire instrument *was* a resonating chamber. If you were to strike the bars of the instrument and lift it at the same time, one could create a complete chamber of resonance and hear a wah-wah sound effect.

With such a unique sound, I was intensely interested in this instrument. When I learned the price was a robust 90€ I decided to wait and see if I could discover it on the internet when I arrived back to the United States. It was cool, and I wanted it, but it was not 90€ cool. Once we returned to the States, I began doing some research and found the hokema sansula kalimba built on a frame drum, used as a sound chamber for vibrato. The instrument was also considerably cheaper, so I did, in fact, take the plunge!

We spent a few hours wandering around the fabulous old streets of Salzburg, before heading back to our hotel. It had been a long, very long day and I was exhausted. The funny thing is, no matter how tired I am, how many miles we drive or how tedious the day is, I still felt energized. The rest didn't matter, as I felt surrounded by my homeland. A place I never lived in but felt like home, each time I returned to Europe.

Oh gosh, tragedy struck!

As we were heading back to the hotel, we realized that we had no wine for our evening routine. How is this possible? No problem, as we planned to pick up a bottle during our walk back to the hotel, that evening.

However, during our walk, we noticed that everything in Salzburg was closed. It was only around 7 p.m., which is considerably early, especially by European standards. *Nothing* was open; no grocery stores, corner stores, and we couldn't find a liquor store anywhere in the area.

We resigned ourselves to the fact we would most likely head down to hotel bar for our nightcap. Sitting at the bar is okay, but it restricts us in so many ways. We can't be in our room, where we can put our feet up, and feel more relaxed.

Just blocks from our hotel, an idea struck. The downside to having a hotel 25 minutes from the old town was the walk and losing the flavor of the old city where we slept. The upside, was that we were just a half a block from the train station and you know what that means, right? Right! There is constant activity at all train stations, no matter what city you visit and I figured that all the shops in the underground would be open.

I was correct in my thinking, and within a few minutes, we had purchased a bottle of wine and some orange juice for Daniel. Along with the thirst quenchers, we picked up an assortment of meats, with a few blocks of cheese, olives, crusty bread and tomatoes. We were content with our purchases and delighted by our discovery.

Back at the hotel, with wine poured, salami residue on our fingertips, we began to think about what to do tomorrow. I powered up my iPad checked the weather in the region. Amazingly, no matter what we decided, no matter where we wanted to go, the skies were forecast to be clear.

My original plan was to stay in Salzburg for three or four nights and take day trips to various local destinations. I knew that regardless of where our adventures took us, there were two absolute musts. The first was to take a short drive directly south of the city to the Eagle's Nest, in Berchtesgaden, Germany. The second was to head a few hours northwest, to the medieval town of Český Krumlov, located in my old stomping ground of The Czech Republic. After consulting with the family, we agreed that our next stop would be in my old neck of the woods. The Czech Republic, here we come.

The Event

Where would I be without Johann Strauss's beautiful 'Blue Danube?' Without this piece of music, I wouldn't be the man I am today. It's a tune that brings out the emotion in everyone and makes them want to waltz. ~Andre Rieu

My phone rang on a Monday night in September 2015. It was a friend calling to say hello, after a long period of silence. After a few kind exchanges of greeting, she got to the real purpose of the call: a friend of hers, Don, was going to be having a New Year's Eve party and wanted to hire an orchestra to play Strauss waltzes into the wee hours of the morning! As a contractor, I have heard a lot of outrageous requests in my life, but this one was close to the top.

When I hung up the phone, I thought that this work might materialize, but because of the scope, I didn't give it much thought for the remainder of the day. Sure enough, the following day, I received an email from Don directly, regarding the matter.

I thought to myself, "It has begun!"

Once Don and I spoke, I had a better understanding of his plan for ringing in the New Year. He wanted to have a significant orchestra perform Strauss Waltzes in a Brooklyn catering hall. Before the party, there would be waltz lessons, and during the bash, he requested background music during dinner. I asked him to send me all his thoughts in an email, so we could start planning the schedule for the evening.

When he followed up, he told me that he was initially considering having the following line up: a conductor, a strings count of six first violins, five second violins, four viola, four cello, three bass, a woodwind section of two flutes, two oboes, two clarinets, two bassoons, a brass section of four horns, three trumpets, three trombones, a tuba as well as a percussionist or two. However, he was open to suggestion and welcomed my recommendations.

As far as the music selection was concerned, he had a few famous waltzes in mind, all at least 10 minutes in length, and wanted to do no more than 15 pieces in total, including the Embassy Waltz from My Fair Lady, My Favorite Things from the Sound of Music, and Someday My Prince Will Com, but gave me total creative licence to add, delete, or alter any of these suggestions.

Finally, Don asked if I could assist him in giving him information on how much space the orchestra would take up, since he needed to know how many risers to get. He also offered to take me to see the space of the venue for myself.

My first impression after reading the email was that I was dealing with a seasoned, older man who was well educated and brought up in a home of culture. Soon, I would have my impression blown with the reality of my client.

Within 24 hours, I responded:

We will need to rent all timpani/percussion equipment required; all the music needs to be either rental or obtained on loan, as well as music stands, chairs (we can use folding), stage, proper lighting. I have included these items in the budget, for your consideration.

We will need a deposit of 110% of the complete budget placed into an escrow account before I can begin working on hiring the orchestra. I will return the unused portion of the deposit by 12/31, before the performance.

Let me know your thoughts and thanks!

Within minutes, Don agreed to the fee, and I knew, I was on my way to one of the largest private events I had ever produced in my career. I began thinking of who would want to work on New Year's Eve, in Brooklyn, and for the fee that I had set up. The answer was easy— everybody!

When hiring musicians, I always think of who my principal players are going to be. Those are the musicians who lead each section. Additionally, I will need to hire a top-notch concertmaster, someone to help lead the complete ensemble. This position is the most vital in the orchestra, and I knew, exactly who I wanted for it. I made the call to my favorite concertmaster, to put in the ask.

Andre and I discussed many aspects of the project and began thinking about who we would ask to conduct the orchestra. Nearly simultaneously, we both paused and realized Andre himself not only could but should, lead the orchestra from the concertmaster position. Instead of sitting on a conventional chair, we decided that he would sit on a high stool, making himself visible to all members. Once we settled on his official duel position, the rest of the details started to come together nicely.

Don and I were communicating about the location of the rehearsal, its runtime, length, musical selections, and many other details of the production. In regards to securing the orchestra, I was on hold, as the bill was large by any standard. It was then that Don asked, "Do you have a PayPal account?" I replied:

Good Morning,
You can send half of the payment now and the other half on December 1. Does that work for you?

Additionally, we need to discuss: music rental, percussion/timpani rental, chairs, stands, and the 7-9 chamber music portion of the evening.

Thank you for allowing me to take on this project. I am incredibly excited and will do everything in my power to contribute to the success of the evening.

A few short hours following that email, half of the deposit showed up in my PayPal account. I was shocked! It was time to roll up my sleeves and get to work.

We were still trying to hammer out certain details of the day. I suggested many different scenarios for him to choose from, which included an orchestra for the three hour rehearsal and three hour performance, a chamber music group A (Octet), a chamber music group B (Harp duo or quartet) and chamber music group C (variety of players)

Logistics:

- Will you be responsible for the musicians' chairs or am I renting them? We will need 45.
- Will you be responsible for music stands? Should we use a folding or rent professional stands?
- Is there sufficient lighting in the Chopin Ballroom for musicians to see their music?
- I will arrange for the timpani and percussion rental by getting three separate estimates and go with the best price.
- Who will be responsible for the final program? I propose allowing Andre and myself to set the program and have you approve it once completed. Does that work for you?
- Dress: I would like you to consider white ties and tails for orchestra men and gowns or very formal wear for orchestra women.

I believe I have covered all the items on my list. Do you have any questions for me? Can you approve the items listed above so I can proceed with my work? ... To be continued.

I soon learned that an event coordinator was overseeing the entire event. With so many details still up in the air, Don and I agreed it would be best if we met at the location for a walkthrough and discussion of all possibilities. The walkthrough with Don, and coordinator Sarah, as well as other friends of Don, took place just a few days later. I must say, seeing is believing!

Seeing and feeling the actual space for the celebration was what we needed. We were able to identify the rooms which the musicians would use, before the rehearsal and during all breaks. We decided on the positioning of the stage (which I still needed to secure). I noted that we would need to acquire music stands, with stand lights. My mind was racing with details dancing around.

Back in my home office, I contacted the best outfit in the tristate area to take care of our stage needs. Freddie Grillson is a seasoned professional, whom I have worked with for many years, on many types of projects. We discussed multiple possibilities and based on those, Freddie began working on budgetary considerations, based on our conversations.

We had all the pieces of the puzzle within our grasp, other than the scores. Where am I going to get the actual parts the musicians will use to perform the event?! Note to self; we need a librarian!

There was only but one call to make, which was to the seasoned professional librarian, Robert Guppy. One of the busiest orchestra librarians in the New York metropolitan area, Robert is the orchestra librarian for the Westchester, Brooklyn, and Long Island Philharmonics, as well as the American Ballet Theatre, and the Colonial Symphony. He has also served in this capacity for the Bard Music Festival, Queens Symphony Orchestra, and Naumburg Orchestra. All of these groups represent what Robert is juggling currently, never mind his incredible past accomplishments.

In the meantime, my phone rang. It was PayPal contacting *me*! They saw large sums of money passing through my account and were calling to learn more about these transactions.

I explained that I have an eccentric client, who wished to use PayPal as their payment method for my consulting work. After a few questions, PayPal accepted the explanation I gave them. I learned that as long as payment was going to a "friend or family," and not for "goods and services," we would have no issues.

I was gathering more details about the musical selections for the main event, as well as those needed for the dance lessons before the party begins. These dance lessons were for Don's guests who desired to learn how to waltz, before the big extravaganza. It seems that Don has thought of every detail. What an extraordinary thinker!

Don had also asked for additional music as his guests are entering the party, they would all be announced, so they could make their grand entrance. The orchestra would perform one work, over and over again, until all of the guests finished entering the main room. With that in mind, Andre, Robert, and I had a conference call to flesh out the details.

"Don, once I get a price on the stage, I will add it to the balance owed," I explained. "For the stage, LED lights, chairs, music stands, stools, and all percussion and timpani set up and delivery, we are looking at additional costs. The stage company has to work out logistics with the hall, so the sooner I have your approval, they can do a walk through at The Grand Prospect.

I got several quotes, and this price is the best available on New Year's Eve. I am seeking your approval ASAP. Off to my 3'o'clock. matinee," At which I received a very simple confirmation, "Done, enjoy your 3 p.m." from him.

His response blew me away; Don was spending a small fortune on this event.

As time progressed, we started to face firm, concrete deadlines. The final program was due, the final stage setup completed, and the final instrumentation organized. There was still much to do. I wrote to Don.

Regarding all the music, I should be able to nail down the musical selections, for both the full orchestra, as well as the chamber players, within two weeks. Will that allow you enough time to get the selections printed for your guests? I am having a blast putting this together.

Over the next few weeks, we made more changes, tweaking the schedule and adding the dance lesson portion. With that addition, I need to consider proper breaks for all the musicians. Some musicians were only performing the rehearsal and performance, and others would be playing the dance portion before the performance. Others still, would be performing background music during the guest's dinner hour.

Don, being the generous guy that he is, informed me that all musicians are welcome to enjoy dinner. There would be an open bar, and the musicians were free to mingle with his guests, as long as they are in tuxedos and or evening gowns.

On November 30, I wrote to my concertmaster/conductor and master librarian:

Here is the final timeline, with my thoughts. Attached is the stage set up that we will be using (this is confirmed). Please see my "pit" style layout and confirm you believe it will work as planned.

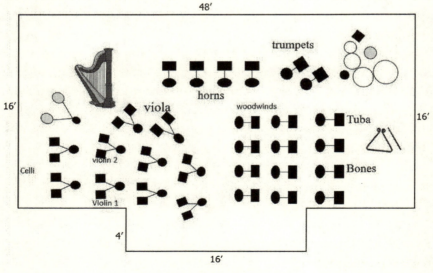

Stage Set Up

Thinking about the flow of the evening, and more importantly, the timing, I have decided that I will not perform in the orchestra. Throughout the evening, I will be talking to Don, and I believe we should be prepared to adjust on the fly. Robert, prepare the full allotment of music with minimal breaks, and we will be ready to cut as/if needed.

I was thinking about what music we should perform as the guests walk in, I had a tune in my head, but couldn't recall the name of the song. I called Robert and sang him the melody that was stuck in my head - I knew it was Mozart, but that was all. After singing a few measures, Robert jumped in and said in the most excited of voice, "That's the Wedding March from The Marriage of Figaro!" Perfect!

The program is complete, all orchestral works, all dance lesson music, as well as our background dinner choices. Just when I thought that my work was completed, I soon learned about another pitfall.

I then received an email from the event coordinator. He had spoken with Freddie during his visit to the hall that day, about the stage setup. The problem was that that they wouldn't be able to access the venue the day before unless they paid to rent the space for the previous day, since the hall wasn't going to be available until noon on the 31st. The coordinator was unsure if Freddie could manage to set up the stage in just three hours, since getting in earlier to set up, you guessed it, would cost them more money.

As if that wasn't bad enough, the stage break down was going to have to take place at 3 a.m. and take no longer than an hour, since the staff closes the building at 4. Oh, and they wouldn't be present to provide any assistance with the process. I couldn't believe this was real. Breaking down at 3 a.m. Really?!

I wrote back, furiously:
Subject: What? Is this for real?

Freddie, is that possible? Please forward the cost for 3 a.m. as well as during normal business hours."

It was time to share this news with Don. I informed him that the hall was only allowing them one hour for the breakdown of the stage and would be charging them twice the double amount for using the crew. I asked him to forward the funds to my PayPal account for the expedited removal and additional labor.

Due to the need to remove the stage, I received my first and only pushback from Don, and rightfully so! He told me that he and a crew of 20 could break down the stage without issue at three and wouldn't even need 50 minutes of the hour to do so. "We've done this kind of thing a zillion times before," he told me with bravado.

The problem with this plan were the liability issues that exist with the stage rental company. I spoke with Freddie, and he was uncomfortable allowing anyone to deal with his stage or crew.

So, I wrote back to Don and expressed my empathy with his concern over the cost and told him that I would proceed as he wished. "Regrets, Don, I didn't see this coming."

Ultimately, Don agreed to the fee, and I had wrapped up another detail for the event.

Now, I needed to make offers to those already hired to perform the regular portion of the evening to play the chamber music works and dance lessons. Here is a sample of my email:

Dear so and so,
During the orchestra "off time," my client would like to have two things happen. One: dance lessons before the main event, for those of his guests who would like to learn the waltz. Two: music during dinner.

I have created a basic outline of our needs. Please let me know if you would be interested in performing at the times indicated below. An additional fee will apply.
1. Dance Lesson 7:00 p.m. - 8:15 p.m. This is a start and stop scenario, with a dance instructor. Maybe 1 or 2 pieces repeated over and over.

Quartet A: 40 minutes
Quartet B: 35 minutes

2. During dinner 9:45 p.m. – 10:30 p.m. (This is not a performance, it is background music)
Quartet B: 30 minutes performs: Haydn Opus 76 #5 and Mendelssohn opus 44 #1

Quartet A: at 10:15 p.m. for 15 minutes (This is not a performance, it is background music) performs *Mozart Dissonance Quartet."*

All of the musicians accepted the additional work. That was the easy part!

On December 27th, I sent the following email to all orchestra members:

Greetings!
All pertinent information regarding the New Year's Eve event is below in this email.

When: December 31, 2015
Rehearsal 3:30-7 p.m. We can enter the Hall starting at 2:30 p.m. The remainder of the evening is below.

Where: Grand Prospect Hall, Brooklyn NY 263 Prospect Ave, Brooklyn, NY 11215 One block from the R train (direct to Times Square, Union Square, etc.). In the **Chopin Ballroom,** I understand that it is possible to find street parking around the hall.

Dress: Ladies, formal Black – Men Tails/White tie

For Music: Please contact our librarian, Robert at R@gmail.com

Payment: For those with PayPal, I have already sent payment. If you did not receive a notification from PayPal, contact me immediately. For those without PayPal, I will have your payment with me on the night of the 31st.

Other: We will supply bass and timpani stools, as well as one for Andre. All musicians will have LED stand lights, as well as music stands. We are having a stage built for the event, but have limited room for set up. We will be setting up as if we were in a theater pit, meaning the strings will be on one side, winds, and brass on the other. Thank you in advance for your flexibility.

TIMELINE and PROGRAM:
7:00. – 8:15: Dance Lessons (chamber players)
7:00 – 7:40: this is a start and stop scenario, with a dance instructor. Quartet A: Music sent.
7:40 – 8:15: Quartet B: MUSIC forthcoming

Dinner for orchestra not involved with dance lessons. I do not know what is on the menu.

8:30-8:45: TUTTI
The Marriage of Figaro - March (repeat as needed)
8:45 - 9:45:
Emperor Waltzes, Wiener Blut (strings), Skaters Waltz, Du und Du (strings), Gold and Silver Waltz, Tales of the Vienna Woods (strings) and Sleeping Beauty Waltz
9:45 - 10:30: – Tutti Orchestra break - while on the orchestra break:
Chamber Music performs
Quartet B: Performs: Haydn opus 76 #5 & Mendelssohn op. 44 #1
Quartet A: Performs: Mozart Dissonance Quartet

10:30 - 11:58
Vienna Bon Bons, Tchaikovsky Serenade Waltz (Strings), España Waltzes, Schatzwalzer (Strings), Swan Lake Waltz, Voices of Spring, Masquerade Waltz, Anitra's Dance, Waltz of the Flowers

12:01 Final Waltz – The Blue Danube

There is a chance we may finish just before midnight, but this will be determined as the night unfolds.
See you on Thursday!

I received a lovely thank you from the violinist who first introduced me to Don, thanking me for putting everything together. She told me the schedule looked "fantastic," which I appreciated.

I wrote her back:
I have spent many hours working on every imaginable detail of this event. It has been a great deal of work BUT, I've been loving every minute!!! Don is one heck of an exceptional guy, and I am certain he will be happy with my work.

Because my wheels were still spinning with possible overlooked details, I decided to also write to the event coordinator to find out if the musicians could leave their cases during the evening and where they'd be able to change into their work clothes, as well as inform her of my arrival time.

Sarah was sure to answer my remaining questions, and now, I felt every detail was in place. But no, as late as the 30th, the emails and details continue:

Freddie, can you add three more chairs, one stool, and four music stands with lights to the order, going to the second floor Grand Ballroom? Instrumentalist require the stands from 7 p.m. to 8:30 p.m.

The event went off without a hitch, and I recorded at least one full hour of video and took over 100 pictures, all commemorating the joyous celebration which brought in 2016. The party was the absolute biggest, most detailed, and spectacular private party I ever had the pleasure of booking.

The guests were all dressed to the hilt. Ladies came dressed in full-length, formal evening attire, with glittery sequins is abundant. The gentlemen were all in black-tie attire, including white gloves and top hat, a truly awesome sight. As the announcer calls out each couple's name, one could hear Mozart playing in the background. The announcer would call out, "Please welcome the honorable, Mr. and Mrs. James Fredrickson," at which point the music would take over upon the couple's entrance into the main ballroom. These introductions lasted for roughly 15 minutes. Once all of the guests had entered the ballroom, the party pushed into high gear.

Each table was set with glass candelabras that held 12 candles, all surrounded by floral arrangements that complimented the delicate lighting. The front of the stage was adorned with over 30 baskets of the most gorgeous, colorful, wonderful smelling flowers I have ever seen. The flower baskets covered the entire 48-foot manmade stage. Astounding!

Don's knowledge of the etiquette in the 19th Century ballroom cannot be understated. Every element of dance carried strict rules of deportment, which he followed to a T. Suggesting the dance lessons before the event only solidifies his strong knowledge.

These lessons proved to be extremely successful, as all of the couples were on the dance floor. As each musical number came to a close, couples would switch partners. Before the next dance selection, the men would bow, while the woman would take a delicate curtsy.

The orchestra played each of the selections on the preprinted dance card, in the order listed. A dance card is typically a booklet displaying all of the dance titles, composers, and the person with whom the woman intended to dance. It would usually feature a cover indicating the sponsoring organization of the ball, as well as a decorative cord by which it may attach to a lady's wrist or ball gown. Don's dance card included both. He also added a small pencil fastened to the card itself, by a second delicate cord. A very classy touch indeed.

The attention Don paid to the extraordinary detail of the ballroom event was unparalleled. I learned that Don was a mere 30 years old. I viewed his as a youngster who is reliving and recreating the art of ballroom dance. Bravo, Don, Bravo!

Once the party was over, I sent Don a word of thanks for the fantastic evening.

Sent: January 2, 2016 1:34 p.m.

Dear Don,
Just a word of thanks for having the orchestra and I play a part in your New Year's Eve gathering. The orchestra members enjoyed themselves

immensely. Your attention to detail didn't go unnoticed by any of us. From the stunning floral selections to the candelabra offering ambiance lighting, photographers in abundance, and the classy touch of dance cards, and we were happy to soak it all in! What A Night!

Thank you for placing your trust in me to produce an orchestra, fit to your needs. I genuinely hope we met or exceeded your expectations.

Sending my best wishes for a happy and healthy new year.

Don's response:

Jim, you nailed it!

Thanks!
Hope to see you soon.

Český Krumlov

"We travel, some of us forever, to seek other states, other lives, other souls." ~Anaïs Nin

August 19 Day 12, 202 kilometers

Although we had driven a long way from Croatia to Salzburg just the day before, I was excited to make the journey back to my other home of the Czech Republic. Just the thought of returning to my adopted hometown brought goosebumps to my arms. Tomorrow's trip would be the first time I have returned to the Czech Republic in more than a decade. I discussed my love for this Country and their people in a chapter of my first book, *Onward and Upward*, in a chapter I affectionately called, "Czech Love." One anecdote I share has to do with obtaining my dual citizenship. In order to purchase a home in the Czech Republic, citizenship is required. I found the perfect apartment, just off of Old Town Square, in the heart of Prague, that I wanted to purchase. Unfortunately, my efforts did not prevail, due to some passport technicalities, but that's a story for another day (that you can read in *Onward and Upward*!

About 130 kilometers into the trip, we found ourselves on the outskirts of Linz, Austria., and were tempted to visit the city. To stop or not to stop?

Linz is the home to the Brucknerhaus, a famous concert hall in the name of Austrian composer, Anton Bruckner. The famous Lentos Art Museum is just up the block from the Brucknerhaus. Another reason to visit is to see the city through the eyes of Wolfgang Mozart. Mozart found the town so inspiring, that during a stopover on his way back home to Vienna in late 1783, he conceived the theme for his Symphony No. 36. Symphony No. 36, "The Linz Symphony." This work gave us serious motivation for a visit. However, I decided I needed to get back to my roots, or, shall I say, my other roots.

Only 40 kilometers from entering the charming village of Český Krumlov, I stepped on the gas pedal a little harder. Crossing the border was simple, as there were no guards, no gate, nothing at all preventing us from entering the country. We sailed across the frontier and, I took a deep breath, as I felt the hair on my back stand up with anticipation.

We followed the A1, until the signs directed us to route 1622. 15 short kilometers later, we took a left onto Kaplická. Now, we are approaching one of the quaintest villages in all of southern Moravia imaginable. I strongly suggest that if you find yourself within a few hours of Český Krumlov, you take advantage and visit. It is well worth it.

Although Earl told us we needed two hours and 25 minutes to complete our journey, he was unfortunately wrong, and it took us about 30 minutes longer than directed. The discrepancy was due to a severely winding one lane road that we were on for the last 20 kilometers of our trip. The speed limit brought us down to 80 kilometers (less than 50 miles per hour) for a chunk of the remaining trip, which also didn't help matters.

When we arrived, nothing looked familiar. Where is my beautiful village that is surrounded by the Vltava?

As we made our way down to the bottom of the elongated hill, everything came into focus, and my memories snapped back to my last visit. On the left-hand side of the car, the village appeared. I was so excited to be so close to the town; I nearly couldn't catch my breath. The excitement was running throughout my body; my heart was beating double time, my eyes were bulging from their sockets, and my memory was ablaze with thoughts.

Consumed by emotions, I couldn't drive another meter, so I stopped on the right side of the road, pretending to see a parking spot. In truth, I needed to regroup so that I could continue driving.

Through tearing eyes, I commented to my family that this wasn't a public parking area and continued down the road. As I flipped the car around, I had a new view of my beloved village and caught sight of one of the staples of the city, the famed bell tower. Surrounding the bell tower are seas of ornate, clay rooftops, which all helped add to the coziness and aesthetically stunning contribution to the skyline. All of these sights and sentiments were alive in my being, and we hadn't even made it into the town yet.

I made a left onto some unknown road, which took us directly to the village. I made it a total of three blocks before the passageway began to close in. The narrowing of the roadway forced me to take left turn to get back to safety. In doing so, we found ourselves within the village walls. From this location, I knew we could walk anywhere we needed; we only need to park the car.

Nearly directly in front of us was an area where only five cars could park. There was one remaining spot vacant, and I took advantage. Something we did not anticipate was the parking instructions being written in Czech, without English translation. Although my knowledge of the Czech language was good at one time, that was nearly a lifetime ago. Russian has been our household language for more than a decade. Just then, a couple who also spoke English appeared and explained to us what was required.

We dropped a 10€ note into the opening, and a receipt came out of the slot, reflecting our payment. We were free to mill about until 6:20 p.m., which should give us more than enough time to enjoy our day and make it back home (to Salzburg) before the wee hours of the night.

We parked at the top of a footbridge which will lead us directly into the heart of town. As we crossed it, the sounds of the city began to come alive. Our parking spot proved to be the ideal location as we were close to everything. I There was so much to take in: there was music playing in the streets, people feet marching on cobblestones, and a plethora of aromas.

We walked through the town to witness first hand all the possibilities of the city. Construction of the town and castle began in the late 13th century, at a fjord in the Vltava River, which was necessary for trade routes in Bohemia. Most of the architecture of the old town dates from the 14th-17th centuries. The town's structures are mostly in Gothic, Renaissance, and Baroque in style. The core of Český Krumlov is within a horseshoe bend of the river, with the old Latrán neighborhood and castle on the other side of the Vltava.

I love it here. I love the energy, the people, and the culture. My memories all came flooding back during the few hours we spent in this incredible scenery. I felt so at home, so at ease. One of the best parts of the experience was the same feeling of joy also being echoed by my wife. I Later, I learned of her excitement about visiting the tranquil little village I loved so much. She too felt what I had experienced so long ago.

What I remember from our first visit may have not been in as accurate as I recalled. But, this time, my memories were in synch with reality.

We spent the next 4 hours walking the streets, eating, taking in the culture, and understanding the history of the people around us. It proved to be the most enjoyable day thus far in our journey. The trip serves as a glorious reminder of a happier time I spent amongst my Czech friends, who I adopted so many years ago.

While reflecting, I came to realize there is no direct correlation between internal wanting and external living. The reality comes from within. I was back in a place where I felt I belonged and could unquestionably adapt too. Why? No idea, some things are better left unexplained. I am sure that if I were to live in this distant land, I would acclimate my habits to fit in with the locals within days. As an American, it is hard to imagine oneself anywhere but in the land of the free and home of the brave. For only the second time in my life, I felt the opposite. That moment, I knew I could be forever a Czech.

By 18:00, it was time to begin our return to our sleeping quarters. Before departing from the United States, I had spoken with a friend who was well versed in travel, who had suggested I make a visit to his "Third most favorite place in the world.". I remembered Strobl was close to Salzburg and also on the way back from the Czech Republic. I plugged in "Strobl," into the GPS and waited for a response from Earl. As it turned out, Strobl was just about on our way back, so we plotted our course and headed south toward Strobl.

Back on Route 1622, head south. We had about 150 kilometers to cover before reaching Strobl, which approximately an hour and 15 minutes. Roughly 45 minutes into the trip, we took an exit off the highway and began our descent into the valley of the Alps.

Near the bottom, deeper in the valley, the scenery became increasingly gorgeous, moving, stunning, and thought-provoking. Adding to the scenic beauty of our journey, was the setting sun. The orange ball just before our eyes was dipping lower and lower behind the towering Alps.

As we moved along this curving road, the sun would peak its head out from time to time, but the sun-rays were omnipresent – just stunning! Eventually, our trip took us deeper into the darkness of the valley. The sun was still up but now blocked entirely by the soaring mountains.

As we came to a juncture in the road, we followed the signs towards Strobl, which indicated 3 kilometers remained. Strobl lies on the eastern side of Lake Wolfgangsee in the Salzkammergut resort region, close to Sankt Gilgen and the Upper Austrian municipalities of St. Wolfgang and Bad Ischl. A small, quaint village-like atmosphere, well worth a visit.

Within a few short minutes, we came to the little town. It was so tiny, that if you hit the gas too hard, you would literally pass through it.

We saw very few lights anywhere, except along the shoreline of Lake Wolfgangsee. It was now about 8:00 p.m. and we were about 40 minutes from Salzburg. There was a small restaurant just ahead of us, so we decided to grab something to eat before making the final leg of our day trip.

We shared a wonderfully warm feast of food and drinks from the region. Simple peasant food: soups, salads, and basic meat dishes, along with house wine and beer from Austria.

We arrived back to our hotel in Salzburg, just before 10:30 p.m. I sat down with my journal and wrote the following sentence: "We had the most beautiful day today, visiting the charming town of Český Krumlov and finishing up on Lake Wolfgangsee in the peaceful town of Strobl. Perfect weather, perfect time together. Perhaps the best day thus far in Europe."

Berchtesgaden

"Not all those who wander are lost." ~J.R.R. Tolkien

August 20 Day 13, 26 kilometers

A short 26-kilometer drive south took us into Germany and to our destination of the day, The Kehlsteinhaus, or in English, "The Eagle's Nest." The Kehlsteinhaus is situated on a ridge atop the Kehlstein, a 1,834-meter sub-peak of the Hoher Göll, rising above the town of Berchtesgaden. This monument was a 50th birthday present given to Adolf Hitler, from the Nazi party, to serve as a place for him to entertain visiting dignitaries.

The four-meter-wide roadway leading to the Kehlsteinhaus ascends some 800 meters over six and a half kilometers. We were already high in the clouds when we reached the entrance of the structure. However, to reach the peak, we walked through a tunnel which leads to an ornate elevator. This will take us the final 124 meters, into the building itself.

The bit of the history that I learned before making the trip helped me to understand in more detail what I was now seeing. Dominating the building's main reception room is an enormous fireplace of red Italian marble. The fireplace was presented to Hitler by the Italian dictator, Benito Mussolini, designed by the Hungarian-born architect, Paul László.

Today, the building is owned by a charitable trust and serves as a restaurant with indoor dining, as well as an outdoor beer garden. It is a popular tourist attraction because of its historical significance of the Eagle's Nest.

The view from the summit took my breath away. We were roughly 2050 meters or 6700 feet in the sky, sharing the same space with the clouds. This stunning backdrop is filled with extraordinary views, fit for a king. History tells us that this was not so, however, as this jaw-dropping location was created for a tyrant. This fact makes the view turned bitter-sweet for this observer. Ultimately, I chose to look at the view from my eyes, with my thoughts, without the history of the person the retreat was built for, but rather, the beauty of the location itself.

We spent a solid hour enjoying our surroundings. I wrote in my travel journal the following: "A 35-minute drive to a most beautiful location, high in the sky, crisp, fresh air, and awesome surroundings. An easy travel day, relaxing drive, easy parking, and wonderful memories were made."

Back in Salzburg, we walked back to the old town. We made our way to the town's central square, to enjoy the scenery. We sat down at a restaurant appropriately called "Triangles.", With a name like that, no wonder we were sitting just across the square from the famed Mozart Festival at the Hofstallgasse. I learned that architect Clemens Holzmeister designed the Großes Festspielhaus (Great Festival Hall) in 1956, for the Salzburg Festival.

As we sat, decompressing from the day's travel, we saw many people dressed in suits and evening gowns. While panning the menu, we continued to see more and more people preparing for the opera, which we learned was slated to begin in roughly 45 minutes.

The hall was just ahead of us on the right. From our seats, we could see the second-floor veranda, where hundreds of people were socializing. It was fascinating to witness the attendees enjoying the final minutes, before the start of the opera. Excitement was in the air, all over classical music, the art of performance. People started lining up, eagerly awaiting to soak in the pending entertainment.

Equally fascinating to both myself and my wife was the attire in which we saw the audience dressed in; everyone was completely decked out. Dressed to perfection in evening gowns, floor-length dresses, tuxedos, seersucker suits, three-piece tailored to perfection ensembles, all with matching shoes, handbags, and jewelry.

All of the outdoor seats in our restaurant was adorned with covers, which looked to be made of a very soft, protective animal skin, possibly cow or bearskin. We found it remarkable that the restaurant owners felt strongly enough to protect those dining in anticipation of the theater, yet to come. They felt the attendees deserve special treatment, to help preserve their beautiful treads. Thus, they covered the seats out of respect to the concertgoer, amazing to us.

Music and the arts are taken very seriously in this area and throughout most of Europe. Even our waiter commented on how many performances take place each day. In his experience, up to three performances of various operas was the daily standard. The passion for live music was abundantly clear to us. Their love for the arts made a powerful impression on our thinking.

If only there were a stronger emphasis on music, theater, dance, the arts here in the United States, perhaps there would be more support for our craft. Music soothes the soul, offers passage to thoughts, and can help calm all those in need. These are some of the qualities that our counterparts in Europe know and understand. Just as I felt my emotions come to life in Český Krumlov, I am reminded of the importance of music while sitting outside at the Triangle restaurant in Salzburg.

A Man Named Ketner

"I was obliged to be industrious. Whoever is equally
industrious will succeed equally well." ~ J.S. Bach

Journal entry, September 15, 2017

During my purging session today, I came across a gem of a find. I unearthed my micro-cassette recorder that I had all the way back in the 90's. Along with the recorder, I also found ten 60 minutes tapes. On these tapes, you could hear me outlining my daily life, feelings, desires, and fears. I heard my thoughts on chance meetings, gigs, apprehensions and so much more.

On one of the tapes, dating back to November of 2004, I spoke about meeting a very influential person, Thomas Ketner, who in the long run, was very helpful in moving my career to a higher level. I would never have known how much this person would do for me all these years later. It is only now, after hearing my voice on the tape that I can share the events I lived through so many years ago.

In November of 2004, I found myself greeting Marvin Hamlisch to our stage at the New Jersey Performing Arts Center. Marvin was a fine gentleman, who seemed to enjoy nothing more than entertaining the masses. He was the guy who wrote *A Chorus Line.* If this was the only work to his name, it would have been more than enough for me to recognize his greatness. When you factor in all of his other accomplishments, it was hard to believe I was sharing the stage with this mega talent. He wrote *The Goodbye Girl, They're Playing Our Song, Jean Seberg, Smile, Sweet Smell of Success,* as well as over 50 works for film.

Once tuning the orchestra and welcoming Marvin to the stage, I ran back to the percussion section, where I was to wear my second hat of the day and start playing. Much to my surprise, Marvin took a seat at the piano, and the conductor entered the stage.

Not knowing who the conductor was, I just sat back and prepared for him to conduct the opening number. He did, and I, along with the rest of the orchestra, played. That scenario repeated itself for about 20 minutes, at which point, the conductor stepped down from the podium, so Hamlisch could take over.

Much to my surprise, he walked over to the percussion section and took a seat just behind my setup. I was stunned, as that is not the most common position for a guest conductor to take. We finished playing the following number when I felt him approaching. He introduced himself, "Hi, my name is Thomas Ketner." His name rang a bell, but in the heat of the day's work, I couldn't place the connection.

After rehearsal, as I was driving home, reliving the day's events. I traced Thomas' introduction back in the percussion section. Ketner, where do I know this name from? Then, BAM, it hit me! Thomas Ketner is one of the most recognized Broadway contractors and music coordinators in the business. His reputation surpasses most, if not all, in his field. He single-handedly negotiated the Broadway terms of what is accepted by one of the most influential unions in North America, The Local in New York City. His Broadway by-laws remain intact to this day. Thomas is an icon in his field, and many look up to him as a revolutionary in our profession.

As if that wasn't enough, Thomas has also been the music contractor for Barbra Streisand, on multiple worldwide tours. Thomas is a man of many talents, all of which are realized at the highest level attainable. The respect he has gained from his colleagues is well earned. Due to his efforts, I learned how to support my players better, promote the working conditions, as well as advocate for all the rights of all musicians.

A few years earlier, I sent a letter of introduction and well as my performing resume to Thomas, for his consideration. I am sure that my resume went into a foot-high pile, filled with all hopeful substitutes who wish to be on his master roster. When I returned to work the next day, I knew I was ready.

Thomas was sitting backstage, waiting for the rehearsal to begin, when I approached him. I mentioned that we had a mutual friend who lived across the street from his home. He replied with a nod of affirmation. I followed up with, "You may recall I sent you my resume some months ago," It was a few years ago, but I felt the need to embellish. Thomas had that blank look on his face, but commented, "Yes, I believe so." A very diplomatic response to my forced question.

Through my contracting position with the New Jersey Performing Arts Center, I had to hire the pit musicians for a run of West Side Story. It is incumbent on me, the music contractor to do due diligence and learn which musicians performed the show while it was running on Broadway.

I learned that Thomas was the music coordinator for West Side Story, as well as so many other shows. This position is a most desirable job in our industry, because of its implications. If *West Side Story* opens on Broadway and Thomas is the Music Coordinator, that meant that he has the rights to the show once it closed on Broadway and began traveling around the world.

Having the "rights," to a show means that you are in control of all the performances, on all continents, as outlined in your agreement. Each theatre must thereby inform each house contractor of the needs of the production. I am the house contractor of the NJPAC and was now in the chain of this particular production.

I found the original roster of musicians who performed West Side Story on Broadway and methodically engaged every one of them for my run at the NJPAC. Using the same players ensured a great musical series, as well as pleasing Thomas Ketner.

I must share that other contractors may have never thought about who played the show on Broadway. Instead, they would have hired their regulars, regardless of the political climate. I was not of that thought process, as I want to please all, as well as gain the trust of those above me. We performed the Hamlisch show without a hitch, and both tucked our newly found relationship into our back pockets.

When will this relationship mature, or better yet, how will it come to fruition? I had no idea, nor did I care. I knew, deep down, that our paths would cross again.

Indeed, as time passed, I proved to be right, as we worked on many more shows together. Between the 25th and 30th performance that I received a phone call from the man himself. "Hey Jim, I am running behind, can you arrange a backstage parking spot for me?" Because of my excellent relationship with the security staff, I asked them for a favor. Thomas then had a sought-after spot waiting for him, next to mine, backstage.

When Thomas arrived, the guards called me. I met him in the parking lot outside, at his designated spot. I greeted him, and as we walked to the theater, he put his hand on my left shoulder and thanked me for taking such good care of him. For me, it was all part of a day's work. For Thomas, it was special treatment.

Once in the building, I offered him a cup of coffee, which he accepted. We then sat down and started chatting. The conversation was unforced and entirely organic. We were having a pleasant conversation about what we did in our field, where and how we started, all of the typical talking points for musicians I did say something to the effect of "In my next life, I want to come back as you!" I remember his response vividly. He said "Me? No way, I want to be *you*!"

Reflecting on that conversation, I soon realized the joke was at my expense. He wanted to be me because he felt I had much more stability in my life, as the personnel manager of the orchestra, as well as the house contractor for the NJPAC. I chuckled hard and told him that whenever he wished to swap places, he should let me know. It is funny how we tend to see each other's lives more clearly than our own.

It was at that moment a thought popped into my mind, which I didn't share with anyone, but logged into my memory bank. "The grass is not always greener on the other side."

Since that realization on both our parts, we have stayed in touch and enjoyed a friendly, as well as professional, relationship over the years.

Fast forwarding to today, I learned that Thomas was preparing to slow down, or dare I say retire, from his Broadway career. Learning this, I became acutely aware that he had realized the absolute pinnacle of success. Thomas was preparing to retire at the ripe old age of 68. Bless you, my friend!

As a result of his imminent retirement, he began to put things into place. Part of that process was to choose a predecessor to take over both his Broadway and off-Broadway work. Part of me wanted the Broadway work that I had experienced through my efforts with *A Tale of Two Cities*, back in 2007. But, I knew better. I was not destined for that line of work. I honestly knew, deep inside, it was not for me. I never shared them with Thomas, though. No need, this is a man who understands without being told.

Thomas had other thoughts, thoughts I had no idea where brewing. What came my way is something that I excel in; legitimate contracting. It was through Thomas that I met my counterparts in France, which secured me to produce for their needs with mega billion-dollar companies, such as *NIKE*, Michelin Tires, and Michael Kors, to name a few. I was ecstatic with my newly found, exciting work.

Later, when I accepted various North American tours, which included *The Legend of Zelda*, *Han Zimmer*, *Game of Thrones*, *Final Fantasy*, and *National Geographic*, I reached out to Thomas to see if he would share some of his local contractor's contact information with me. I knew he had covered pretty much every city, in his tours with Streisand. Much to my surprise, Thomas offered me every contact in every city I requested.

To this day, I am using his Rolodex I proudly share our close relationship with all of his connections.

Innsbruck

"Travel far enough you meet yourself." ~David Mitchell

August 21 Day 14, 187 kilometers

I had mixed emotions about heading to Innsbruck. On the one hand, it is a gorgeous city, located in the valley between the high mountains of the North Chain in the Karwendel Alps and the Patscherkofel and Serles to the south. On the other, Innsbruck is the penultimate European city on our mini-tour. I began to feel the unmistakable sadness that tortures me towards the end of every trip. I adore Europe—her sights, tastes, feel, and the fantastic people we encounter along the way. I often fantasize about staying here longer than the precious few weeks of our holidays.

We were now on the A8, heading west toward the A12 which will take us from Salzburg to Innsbruck in about 2 hours. This time, Earl was correct in his calculation. We would spend three short days and two nights in Innsbruck, before heading back to Zurich for the final night of our trip. Our 3300-kilometer circle would be complete, as we would end up in the city where we started, while retracing our steps in the Czech Republic.

As a family, we have experienced so much, so many beautiful sights over the past few weeks. So much was absorbed, understood, and lived. We really did it all. Our visit to numerous lakes, the Adriatic and Mediterranean Seas, the Swiss, Italian, and Austrian Alps, all equally breathtaking. We spent the currencies of the dollar, Euro, Koruna, Swiss Franc, and the famous Kuna of Croatia. There was water with and without gas, red and white wine, light and dark beer. Pasta, pizza, fish, meats, salamis, cheeses, bread both plain and stuffed, pastries of every type, tomatoes, pickles, olives both pitted and not, fruits, and more. We traveled via airplane, airport shuttle, car, bus, funicular, water boat, Vaporetto, train, and cable car, across the seven countries we visited. The circle included some perfect tangents, allowing us to divert from our perfect circle, to take in some fantastic discoveries. What an easy-going family I have, willing to make the extra effort to see what most may have missed.

Back in Innsbruck, we were happy to hear and use the more familiar Italian language. Music to my ears, especially after our bout with the German language, of which I understand next to nothing.

Once settled into our new home at the Best Western Hotel Mondschein, we ventured out to have a first look at the town and grab a bite to eat. We stumbled onto a Pizzeria, of all places, but this one claimed to be, "The best in Innsbruck." What choice did we have?

We took a look at the menu and placed our order. As we sat amongst the other patrons, the other tables all around us began to fill up. Directly to my left was a table of four, with two older men, and two younger men, about my age. To my right were four children, all around 15 years old. Directly behind me were two women, apparently the wives of the men my age, and two younger women.

It was not difficult for us to see that this was a group of friends, or quite possibly, a large family. This became more apparent, as I observed the men break out into what appeared to be a natural after-dinner ritual of cigar smoking.

The oldest of the group caught my eye, as he lit his quarter size offering. I nodded at him approvingly, as the tip of the cigar came to a familiar glow. He nodded back and offered his open case to me, which was filled with short cigarillos. I have not smoked in years, so I declined, waving my hand right to left. He nodded silently in affirmation.

A little later, after espresso, we were in full relaxation mode. The second man who sat at the table across from me noticed I was nodding off. I guess the car ride to Innsbruck had caught up with me. Added to the fatigue of travel was a half-liter of rose, my body and mind required some rest. It felt like the perfect time to take a siesta.

Somewhat embarrassed that he caught me zoning out, I looked at him and said "Ho sonno," I am exhausted. Both men chuckled with understanding. I took that as an opportunity to strike up a conversation.

I began by thanking them for offering me a cigar a short while ago. One man told me, it is not just any cigar, but one of the varieties which we make in Tuscany. As much as my heart wanted to share in this treat, my resolve declined a second time. I explained the best I could that I had quit smoking many years ago and couldn't go back now. They nodded again with understanding.

Our conversation continued, as we discussed topics ranging from family life, to travel, music, my brother John who passed in 2010, Francesco Paolo Neglia, and more. When I made statements about "La Famiglia," my new friend would turn to his 13, 16 and 19 years old daughters and restate the meaning behind the term.

The kids sat there like portraits, listening, absorbing what their father Pietro had to say. I was amazed at their depth, curiosity, and desire to understand their Papa. Pietro's 19-year-old daughter, Giuliana, seemed to be following in her parent's footsteps. She was confirming what her father was speaking to her younger siblings. It was adorable for me to witness this caring family sharing stories of love and concern, with the next generation. I felt the depth of my heritage coming through from Giuliana and Pietro.

The older man sitting on the right side of Pietro spoke of his two brothers back home and how they still shared their sincere belief in the importance of family ties. La Bella Vita was a theme throughout our conversation.

The topic of discussion shifted to the importance of music and the arts and how they impact our lives for the better. As the dialogue sunk deeper into more nuanced words, my limited Italian language skills prevented me from giving a detailed response, just as Pietro's limited English skills became clear. Yet, we continued.

I learned Giuliana played the flute and that Pietro had played the piano, but stopped studying long ago. "When she gets older, she will regret stopping or not pursuing her love," he told me. At his age, he is beyond regret, as it is too late to go back and start over.

Since smelling the aroma of the first cigar, Phillip was on a mission. Without telling me verbally, I knew where he was going. By the time this part of the conversation was taking place, Phillip had returned from his cigar run. Cubans were legal and available in Europe, and Phillip was sure to take advantage.

Pietro asked me, "Quanti anni ha tuo figlio?" or "How old is your son?" 19 years, I told him. "Ah, just like my daughter!" he exclaimed. "I know you and your wife play music for your life and living, what does Phillip play?" Now, Phil had a decent command of the Italian language and answered for himself. "I used to play piano and trumpet." You could hear in Phillips' voice that he had apparent regrets in not continuing his studies.

Pietro picked up on it and said, "If you regret at 19, it is one thing, but to regret when you are an old man like me, you will learn all about serious regret. A regret which doesn't go away, ever." The conversation deepened and moved toward family importance once again. Pietro and I locked eyes with what felt to be a complete understanding. What a moment, a moment emblazoned in my mind, my thoughts and now my journal.

Although we had a language barrier between us, we overcame it. I felt this man understood me and all I represented as both a man and a father. As the evening came to an end, we exchanged email addresses, in the hope that we would continue our conversation and friendship.

Simpatico in our views, morals, and upbringing, thus creating memories that will last a lifetime.

The Day Of

"Laughter and tears are both responses to frustration and exhaustion. I myself prefer to laugh since there is less cleaning up to do afterward." ~Kurt Vonnegut

Journal entry, March 1, 2017

As I reflect on the past few weeks of the continuous movement, work, and life, I must share the following account of the events, which peaked on Sunday, February 12, 2017.

A symphony pop concert was set to begin at 3 p.m. at the State Theater in New Brunswick, New Jersey. Sasha and I live about 40 minutes from the theater, a venue we perform at regularly. A 1:15 p.m. departure is standard for a 2 p.m. arrival, but as personnel manager, I always attempt to arrive an hour before the official start time for all services.

That afternoon my wife asked me if I would drive to work, much to my surprise. No problem, I confirmed I would take the wheel on this trip. How strange, I thought to myself, as Sasha drove more than 90 percent of the time, but on this day, she passed on the responsibilities to me.

Heading south on Route 287, I began to feel as if the weight of the world was on my shoulders, or worse yet, my chest. I am sure this feeling is brought on by the thought of all the projects that were still sitting on my desk, all the responsibilities waiting for me, all the pressure, and details starring me in the eye. But the worse pressure is the nervousness of completing the mountain of work on my desk in a timely fashion. I was overwhelmed with rapid firing thoughts, as I couldn't avoid the pressure of the workload.

We were silent in the car, both of us wrapped up in our thoughts. That is a rare occurrence, as Sasha and I always enjoy chatty car rides. When we were about five minutes from our exit, I shared with my wife what was on my mind. "I am in severe pain, and my chest hurts. I think I should get checked out by a doctor," I said to her.

Without missing a beat, she entered "Hospital" into our working Waze navigation program. She found that we were about a mile or so away from the closest hospital. Sasha pleaded with me to pull over so she could drive, but I declined. At the time, I didn't offer her an explanation, but a few hours later I shared with her why I continued to drive I feared if I let go of the control of the car, I would have a heart attack. I was sure that if I remain focused on the drive, I could ward off what I was certain to come. Yes, I was scared, and this time, it was real.

As we pulled into the emergency entrance of Robert Wood Johnson Hospital, I jumped out of the car and asked Sasha to park and meet me inside. Once out of the car, a real fear shower over me, I lost my balance and nearly fell to the ground.

I hobbled through the electronically opening doors. The administrator at the desk asked if I was okay. "No, my chest is heavy, and I'm scared." Before I could say another word, I was placed on a gurney and wheeled into a waiting team of nurses and doctors.

In the blink of an eye, my shirt was off, and adhesive applicators were placed strategically on my body. Seconds later, a nurse began an EKG, measuring my heart's electrical activity. The acting physician informed me that they needed to run more tests while they were waiting for the results of the EKG. One of the nurses placed a nitroglycerin patch on my chest and told me that I might experience a sharp headache, as they are one of the more common side effects of the patch.

It is now 2 p.m., and our performance was set to begin in an hour. In a moment of delirium, I asked the nurse if I would be released soon as we needed to get to the State Theater for our 3 p.m. performance. The nurse informed me quite definitively that I wasn't going anywhere, anytime soon. I didn't have the energy to argue. At that moment, Sasha arrived after parking the car.

I tried to process what was happening but struggled to digest even basic observations. I thought I knew where I was. I believed I was in the hospital but was not sure of why? The nitroglycerin was working. Another set of side effect of absorption were slight disorientation. I didn't realize that part until the following day when I attempted to document the events of my visit.

In a moment of clarity, I asked Sasha to call three people: a coworker on the operations team who was running the performance, the assistant personnel manager, and one of the members of the percussion section. I also asked her to please only inform the operations manager that I was in the hospital. As for my assistant personnel manager and percussionist, Sasha simply stated that I wasn't feeling well and she needed to take me back home. Sasha asked my operations partner to keep the phone call confidential, as I didn't want anyone to know that I was weak or ill. Weakness is viewed as a detriment to life, especially in my line of work.

Once Sasha had informed them, I began to settle down. Although I had never missed a day of work, I was instantly relieved. Thinking It was the doctors who forced me to take the concert off, it wasn't my choice! Still, I was overwhelmed with concern, for myself this time, not the life of my colleagues or musicians. My God, what is happening and why?

The first time the doctors measured my blood pressure, it was high. However, the doctors attributed that to my fear and the pending performance that I was about to miss.

Things in the hospital were moving very quickly, faster than I had ever seen in my lifetime. Nurses, doctors, and staff all working to ensure my safety. I became overwhelmed by the caring team and could feel my eyes welling up.

Minutes later, I was hooked up to a machine that would begin monitoring my every heartbeat, movement, pulse, and blood pressure. Additionally, a nurse started an intravenous in my right arm. I do recall that the poor nurse failed twice with my left arm, which is when I suggested trying my juicier right side. Success!

Blood test after blood test took place, which each requiring a two-hour waiting period for results. The tests took place over three multi-hour cycles. During one of these, my blood pressure dropped to a normal, acceptable level. The attending physician shared the findings with us, after each test cycle. All of the results were negative. The doctors were baffled by my current condition as I was in their words, "The picture of health."

Nearly eight hours have passed since I entered the building and the doctors found no reason to hold me, except one. They wanted me to stay overnight, so that they could perform what was felt to be a crucial stress test, in the morning. We had to make a decision. Should I spend the night and have a stress test in the morning at the hospital, or go home now and schedule it with my regular cardiologist, later. After some discussion, we agreed on the second option

Happy to be released from the hospital, but struggling to come to grips with what frightened me so much on the trip to New Brunswick, I was still in search of answers as to why this had happened in the first place.

The doctors were perplexed as well, as they struggled to pinpoint a specific cause of my discomfort. How could someone with no signs of any heart stress or blood pressure issues experience such pain?

The nurses and doctors were taking notes on my medical history.

They asked questions regarding my family history, as well as specific questions about my home and work life. They began to probe into my personal life, what I did each day, my exercise regime, and any other stressors in my life worth mentioning. The staff was, at the very least, thorough.

Just before 10 p.m., the head nurse entered our room to share the final diagnosis, obtained by a unified team of doctors. When they learned of my work schedule and how much I was balancing, as well as how few hours I was sleeping each evening, the consensus was not only clear, it was apparent. I was suffering from exhaustion and needed to take rest and do whatever is required to change my current course of life, or else, experience permanent ramifications.

Stress and exhaustion have different forms of manifestation, which vary from person to person. Mine reared its ugly head as an incredible pressure on my chest. During this time, I never had difficulties breathing, or catching my breath, but the heaviness in my chest was as real as can be.

While waiting for our release from the hospital, I asked my wife to hand me my phone. She told me that I wasn't allowed to check email for a week.

I agreed with her. Instead of checking email, I moved my thumb toward the camera app. Once opened I snapped a hospital selfie. This picture would serve as a reminder of how I never wanted to look again.

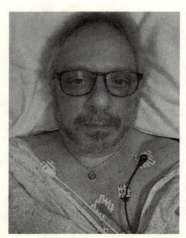

Right eye smaller than the left – the look of fear 2/12/17

This time, I was lucky, extremely fortunate. I learned two significant bits of information on that horrible Sunday. First, according to all the test and doctors' reports, I was healthy and did not have a heart attack. Secondly, the episode was as a wakeup call, a that I couldn't ignore. For that recognition and understanding, I am grateful.

Earlier in the day, there was a period where I thought I might be checking out, permanently. Dying scared the heck out of me, as I was nowhere near ready to throw in the towel. I am grateful for the second chance, one I wish not to screw up.

There is a price to pay for live a lifestyle like mine, but it also forces me to remember that we are all humble and fragile. There is a vulnerability to all of us.

Time to reflect.

Nordkettenbahnen

"I read; I travel; I become" ~Derek Walcott

August 22 Day 15, 1.4 kilometers

I laughed out loud. I mean, have you read the past 20,000-word account of this trip? My poor pencil is a mere nub.

We had made no real plans for the day so that we could use it to relax, and unwind from the past few weeks of traveling. After Googling "Side trips from Innsbruck," we chose something a little different and decided to discover the Nordkettenbahnen.

The best way to climb Innsbruck's majestic Nordkette mountain range is to step aboard the Nordkette cable car. This will take you to towering heights, with the most fantastic views. The Nordkettenbahnen will take us directly from the city center to high mountain terrain in about 20 minutes.

We boarded the "Seegrube" and rose to just over 6,000 feet. Here, we saw views of the middle Inn Valley, the Stubai, Zillertal Valley Alps, and the Wipptal Valley, all the way into Italy. It was time to sit, relax and enjoy the view. So, we had lunch at the Alpenlounge Seegrube, where you have a front-row view of grandeur.

Atop the Nordkette, we found the best panoramic views of Innsbruck and the surrounding areas. If this wasn't high enough, there is the option to go higher, to the Hafelekar. Seeing signs for the Hafelekar; we continue up to the next level to the 7,600-foot peak, the highest viewpoint available to us. The visual contrasts between the mini-city below and the opulence of the mountains make for long-lasting memories, impossible to forget.

As we began our long ascent in the suspended cable car, I was visibly shaking from the heights surrounding us. Everyone in my family knows I suffer from acrophobia and this trip only confirmed their beliefs. Although this is one of my many faults, I was able to withstand the descent, wobbly legs and all. The trip down and the scenery surrounding embraced me, so much so, that I was able to take pictures to commemorate the occasion. I wanted to showcase how I was attempting to overcome my fears.

Although I was doing a decent job conquering my fears, the truth is, I felt sick to my stomach as a result of the heights. I was terrified and hanging on the steadying grips hanging from the ceiling like an oxygen mask.

Once back in town, and after kissing the steady ground, we looked for a place to enjoy our final meal in Innsbruck. I recall having had sea bass, spätzle, and vegetables. I noted in my journal "Mission accomplished, fish and spätzle remained in my stomach, even after the terrifying ordeal of the Nordkette cable car ride." Another item checked off of my bucket list!

Paying Your Dues

"I work very hard, and I play very hard. I'm grateful for life. And I live it - I believe life loves the lover of it. I live it." ~Maya Angelou

While I was proofreading the stories in this book, I came to realize that most of what I do in my professional life has to do with details, specifically the execution of those details. Similarly, as a percussionist, it is my responsibility to dissect each part assigned to me and prepare it, so I can execute the music at a professional performance level. That means thinking about every note in the score and how I can contribute to the overall performance.

Many of the instruments in the percussion family are not pitched, or are non-melodic, for those passages, my concentration turns more so to execution. How shall I phrase the part? Perhaps a complete non-pitched passage is written in a mezzo forte dynamic, mezzo forte meaning medium loud. If that were the case, I might start out just a little softer than mezzo forte and crescendo too, or just above mezzo forte, to help create a tension that will help propel the theme. Or, maybe a musical motif to an unwritten feeling. Creating tension allows us to insert our part in a viable way. Instead of executing a passage flat (without motion), phrasing, the dynamic range will almost always please the music director and enhance the overall performance.

It is our duty as percussionists to color and highlight the musical landscape, to heighten each passage with our interjections, and contribute by using the tools afforded to us. The direction I choose will need to fit into how the conductor envisions the passage. So, when preparing, I always keep several possibilities in my back pocket. I base these possibilities on my preparation, belief, and execution of the particular passage. The rest is up to the person at the podium.

If there are multiple instruments to cover on a given work, such as xylophone, snare drum, castanets, tambourine suspended cymbal and triangle, that adds another level of preparation. I need to consider getting from one instrument to another, with complete freedom and flexibility.

These examples are just the beginning of what we must be aware of on a daily basis, during our work life both on the stage and in the practice room. This is what goes into the endless amount of mental and, in many cases, physical preparation, for a week of work at the symphony.

While wearing my other hat, it is incumbent on me as a contractor, to think about every possible aspect of each event. Each service carries a unique footprint of needs and requirements; the circumstances of each unfold as each service takes place.

When working on each gig, I am always acutely aware that there is some disaster just waiting to happen. My job is to ensure that there are no disasters. In fact, it is my responsibility to lay out each project and dissect it from start to finish. When looking at each series, I carefully think about what may happen at each service. Moreover, I must predict and head off what pitfalls *may* occur and prevent the production from imminent disaster.

I could fill a complete book outlining all of the problems which have caused me considerable issues in the past, both mild and severe mishaps. Conversely, I have dealt with issues that nearly caused the demise of a given service. But I was able to see the issue coming. Better yet, I was able to shut it down before it came even close to materializing. That is a true art, a gift, an awareness or what I came to call my sixth sense.

As the years have progressed, the easier it has been to ward off potential problems. Experience is something that only comes with time, age, and countless mishaps along the way. I have taken all the past experiences, good and bad, and learned from them. Lessons that one would never consider being a possibility in life, all became second nature to me.

I have experienced all sorts of problems, including, but certainly not limited to, a harpist showing up to work without their harp! Yes, that has happened to me and has happened to other players as well, from an oboist to cellist, all forgetting their instruments on a concert day. I have had players who forgot their auxiliary instrument, (meaning, the Bb clarinet player who needs to play on an Eb clarinet as well, forgot their Eb instrument at home).

I have been in positions where we were just 40 minutes away from the start of a rehearsal and a key player called to say they would be late. I'm not talking five minutes late, but an hour, sometimes more, up to an hour or more. Resolving these types of issues is a multitiered process, starting with high volume phone calls, followed by complete disclosure of the problem to the music director or visiting conductor.

In true emergency cases such as this, I go to my trusty iPhone and hit "Trumpet." Within seconds, every trumpet player in my database pops up. Not only did I program my iPhone to show me their phone number, but also, their geographic location. The player with the closest address to the site of the rehearsal receives the first call.

Now, in 2017, I have learned that I can send out a group text blast to find an available substitute, which saves me a great deal of time on the phone. In our area, musicians are hungry and wish to work. A text blast stating "Emergency, the first to respond gets the work," followed by the particulars, usually yields an available player.

What I have learned as personnel manager and contractor alike, is that it is my complete and sole responsibility for anything and everything, that happens on the stage during the parameters of every service of the orchestra. Yes, a massive responsibility.

Managing is an art. Like any great work, it becomes more valuable over time.

While sharing my thoughts on being a personnel manager, I feel compelled to share another side of my thinking, A part that, over the years, has proven to be an enormous part of my overall thinking and approach.

I am always downsizing, purging things from our home, my office, and our lives. Recently, while looking through some tucked away boxes, I stumbled across a fascinating find— all of my past agenda books. Each year is represented, from 1988 through 2017, waiting for further inspection.

I couldn't help but think about Ray's red journals and the advice he offered me nearly three decades ago. "Jim, keep a written record of all those events you feel are worthy of noting." Well, I did just that. I followed Ray's advice and wrote and wrote over the years. So many details documented, most of which came alive during this purging session. I have the privilege of reliving and sharing those stories with you now, in between the covers of this book.

After peering through the pages of my past date books, there is no mistaking why I feel I have put a lifetime of effort, over the past 30 years. As I sifted through the 1988 agenda, I took note of what sort of work I was committed to, during that year.

As I looked forward, I began to see a thread of what work repeated and what new jobs were coming in. I found that aspect of my past agendas most telling. I read on, page after page, year after year. I was stunned to see how many groups, ensembles, orchestras, and gigs I came across during my career. It was very impressive.

While sifting through the agendas, many memories came flooding back. In some cases, the thought of the numerous commutes to gig after gig, most notably the commute from my New Jersey home in North Arlington to the State Capitol of Harrisburg, Pennsylvania. Looking forward, the reality of travel from city to city, moved from country to country. More memories became prevalent, which only brought back powerful stories from foreign trips, performances, experiences.

Hours of thumbing through the books also yielded a partial list of the organizations which played a contributing role in assisting me to arrive at the life I enjoy today. I share the list only to recognize all those who have in some way, be it large or small, contributed to my life's journey.

I remember the countless commutes to and from work vividly. The route most emblazoned in my memory is the route I drove to Harrisburg, Pennsylvania, 80 times per year. That commute took place for about eight years, and the drive was a grueling 180 miles each way.

A decade with the Queen's Philharmonic, High School musicals throughout New Jersey, Graduations at every possible college in New York, New Jersey, and Pennsylvania, Stamford Symphony, more commuting to Connecticut, New Age ensemble rehearsals and performances.

As a side job, I learned how to tune and recondition pianos. I spent a better part of ten years working that trade. There was the local drumline coaching at various high school: Hunter College Playhouse LOOM (Light Opera of Manhattan). As if that wasn't enough on August 1, 1989, I purchased my first house. Coaching at the Youth Symphony, work studies at Mannes, my church gig, Staten Island Symphony, The Adelphi Symphony, Westchester Philharmonic, Ethos percussion quartet, Christmas and holiday gigs, teaching lessons, Solid Brass performances and tours, Ringling Brothers Circus, St. Peter's by the Sea orchestra (which had a schedule of 30 plus performances each December), Long Island Symphony, Princeton Pro Musica, Princeton Symphony, Summer Opera at the Paramount Theater, Asbury Park, various wedding bands, Bridgeport Symphony, Czech Radio Symphony, New Philharmonic of NJ, Scranton Symphony/Northeast

Philharmonic, Wayne Chamber Orchestra, The Plainfield Symphony, Greenwich Symphony, Berkshire Opera, Morristown Choral Society, Amore Artis, Ars Musica, 11 years at New Jersey State University, AMDA, Masterworks, Wanita's Dance Company, St. Patrick's Cathedral, Young Audience Percussion Trio, New York City Opera, Perform America, Pro Arte Chorale, New York Chamber Symphony, Oratorio Singers of Westfield, Riverside Symphonia, Westminster College Choir, Field Studies International, Tale of Two Cities, Disenchanted the Musical, NIKE, Michelin Tires, Michael Kors, Perform America, Johnny Mathis, Joan Rivers, Spike Lee, Perspectives Ensemble, Mario Cantone, New York Pops, GBP Live, AWR Music, American Symphony Orchestra, Teatro Grattacielo, Szentendre Chamber Orchestra, Saint Cecilia Symphony, and so on and so on.

There were years where I didn't have two consecutive days off, until August. The work was plentiful. In fact, there was so much work, that it was impossible to accept everything I was offered. There just wasn't enough time in the day to cram it all in.

Zurich

"It is good to have an end to journey toward; but it is the journey that matters, in the end." ~Ursula K. Le Guin

August 23 Day 16, 286 kilometers - Circle complete.

Typically, a three-hour trip doesn't cause me any anxiety. However, due to the pouring rain, the drive from Innsbruck back to Zurich falls under the category of white-knuckle driving. Just as we entered the Country in the rain, a few weeks earlier, so shall we enter again. We had a long, tedious drive ahead of us, heading westward on the E60.

While driving this final leg of our trip, I kept in mind what I have tucked in my proverbial back pocket for weeks. That memory translated directly to "Gas up before coming back to Switzerland because the diesel is costly there."

Roughly two and a half hours into our trip, just before the Hohenemser Strasse, we pulled into a service station to off our tank. The total cost was a whopping 45€. I would repeat the same process as we neared the airport but hoped to pay only 15 Swiss Francs.

Approaching the city limits, Earl indicated we were just five minutes from our hotel in downtown Zurich. Not only was I excited to be arriving, but I was also relieved that this was the final drive of our European tour. Somewhere deep inside, I was rejoicing.

The odometer read 9570 KLM, which means we drove a total of 3118 kilometers (1937 miles) during our journey. Every kilometer worth it, every moment, memorable.

Once again, the weather gods were on our side. Just before crossing into Switzerland, the dark rain clouds made a halt in between the last mountain chain and the approaching tunnel; there wasn't one dark cloud on the horizon. Clear skies welcomed us across the Austrian-Swiss border.

Come to think of it, there was only one occasion where the weather turned nasty. It was during our final night in Innsbruck, just after we'd finished dinner when it looked like it was going to rain. We were only a few blocks away from our hotel, so we decided to go back and grab our umbrellas. Suddenly, the skies darkened quickly before our eyes, and the wind started to howl.

We needed to cross the Danube, to reach our hotel on the other side. While we were on the bridge, waiting for the light to change, I lifted my head to grab a glimpse of the Alps. All of a sudden, an enormous lightning bolt lit up the sky. It was a truly a breathtaking, yet frightening, sight. The burst of light highlighted the Alps and their complete magnificence. Just as we crossed the bridge, waiting for the final light to signal our safe passage, the sky opened up. Let it rain!

We arrived at our Zurich hotel before our 2:00 p.m. check-in time. After leaving our luggage with the concierge, we ventured out of the hotel's vicinity. What should we do? We had just one day to catch a glimpse of the 35-square mile city.

The nearly immediate consensus was to visit the Altstadt, or Old Town. We took a leisurely pace to the Altstadt, which hosted plenty of sites to see during our relaxed tour. We enjoyed Lindenhof Hill, St. Peter Kirche, and the 9th-century Fraumunster church. Crossing the Limmat River, we stumbled upon the unique Kunsthaus art museum.

We were sure to take as many breaks as were needed. Our European trip was coming to an end, and we were all feeling the full effects of fatigue setting in.

During our stroll, we found ourselves on Napfgasse, only steps away from one of the best cafés in the old town, Café Schober. This café was established in 1845 and legend has it that all of their success has been due to their tasty, addictive selection of 'favorites.'

At the top of the list is the Schoggi Mélange, better known as fancy hot chocolate. The smell of the fresh kugelhopf, Bundt cake, and apple swirls, the sight of the truffles and pralines, and almond dragees. There was also incredible looking Spitzwegerich-Zältli, or sweet drops, and Züri-Hüppen, also known as honey cookies filled with cream. So many choices!

Our walk took us through nearly all of the one and four downtown districts. The sun began to set during our walk Just around the corner from our hotel on Römergasse 7, we came across a well-known restaurant. It was here, at the Le Dézaley, we would share our final dinner of the trip.

Le Dézaley has an extensive menu, which is accompanied by a superb wine list. Once settled in, we made our choices. For starters, we enjoyed platte Waadtländer Rohschinken (or air-dried ham board) from Vaud, and an order of 12 escargots.

For our entrée, we enjoyed Gemischte Platte mit Trockenfleisch für 2 Personen, which are air-dried meats, meant for two people. Not being a big meat eater, I decided on the Egli filets in butter gebraten mit zitrone und mandeln (or Perch Fillets), grilled with lemon and almonds. Daniel also rocked the fondue au fromage.

We then decided to order two bottles of wine, one red for the meat eaters and one white for the fish eater (that would be me). Both were local wines, which the establishment boasts as "parfait," or perfect for our meal.

While lying in bed later that evening, I began to prepare for the travel day ahead. The thought of leaving the European continent caused me to sink into my unavoidable ways. I began to feel empty, hollow, with the familiar signs of depression starting to hit.

As I forced my tears back, closing my eyelids as firmly as possible, I hoped I could sleep. I began to think about our next trip, our next destination, our next home away from home, and my tears began to dry up.

Final Hours in Zurich

Liberation

"There's a little bit of pain in every transition, but we can't let that stop us from making it. If we did, we'd never make any progress at all."
~Phil Schiller

In August 2017, towards the beginning of what would have been my fourteenth year as personnel manager with the New Jersey Symphony Orchestra, I found myself in the most reflective mood. I was on a trip to Scandinavia when this mood set in. Not only was I deep within the fjords, but I also found myself deeply absorbed in personal thoughts.

"Norse Fjörðr," or Norwegian Fjord, in English, means "Where you travel across," or, something more appropriate to my current situation, "Å sette over på den andre siden" in English means "Put across to the other side."

While sitting on the shoreline in Geiranger, Norway, enjoying the awesomeness surrounding me, I had an 'aha' moment or more so a *à sette over på den andre siden* moment. I was enjoying the fresh, crisp air, the graffiti-free Country, the knowledge of free healthcare, retirement communities which were entirely funded by the government, no homeless on the streets, breathing in the cool air, deep within the majestic fjords. The feeling of a slower paced life was overwhelming to comprehend. My thinking began to change.

During our trip, I learned that native Norwegians like to hike as a form of relaxation. The natives live what I perceive as a stress-free lifestyle. All of these thoughts were swirling around in my head, at this particular moment in time. These collective thoughts began to make an impact on me, on my emotions, and subsequently, my life.

The burning thought that consumed my mind was how I could get out of the fast-paced, hectic American lifestyle which has engulfed me all these years, while maintaining a lifestyle we have grown accustomed. How can I live my life at a much slower, more regular pace, offering me a life of less? These life-altering thoughts, along with my hearing deterioration, helped to push me towards the only logical conclusion. I needed to start putting an ending to this chapter of my life.

With the future in my sights, I pressed the mental pause button on my thoughts, as I needed to take the time to digest and process the outcome of this possible change. Did our incredible surroundings propel my decision or thoughts? Did Norway have some influence on my decision, or did Geiranger catalyze what I have been contemplating for the past few years? I believe all of my thoughts to be real and part of the guiding force moving me to the ultimate decision. What an eye-opening vacation!

Leaving the symphony has another repercussion in my life, as this decision affects not only me but also my marriage. Sasha is still a member of the orchestra, and we have worked together since we met, decades ago. If I left, she would go to work on her own, and this carries many implications and changes for our functioning us as a couple. We enjoyed our work life, as well as our home life together.

Daily, our alarm would sound, and after we would have a cup of coffee then got into the car and headed East on route 280. Once at the NJPAC, we would partake in our rehearsal schedule. After rehearsal was over, we would drive home and continue our evening with our sons, tending to their activities and needs. There was a rhythm to our lives, which defined us, to a certain extent. All of that was on the line. There was a great deal to consider.

The Ugly Truth

Tough times never last, but tough people do.
~Robert H. Schuller

Personnel managing requires a certain finesse, a finesse that most in our field do not acquire in a lifetime of work. That is not to say I am better than most, or even some, because I am not. However, what I do have are the proper instincts it takes to get a very tricky job done, with complete delicacy. Experience is non-transferable, so my knowledge of personnel managing comes exclusively from years of hands-on experience.

Part of my job, although not part of the job description, is to ward off issues before they rear their ugly head. Throughout my career, I learned how to shut down most problems before they even come to the surface.

Over the years, I have learned that equally crucial to working with an offended player is to share the more significant issues behind the scenes with the orchestra committee, gaining their thoughts, views, and hopefully, their support.

An orchestra committee consists of an elected governing body of musicians, placed into power by the membership itself. Every orchestra has guidelines on how long a committee or council can be in place, before the next election cycle. I have learned that a competent working committee is integral to the success of any organization and that my relationship with the committee is an invaluable one.

When a new committee is first elected, it is my tradition to let a few days to pass before starting a dialogue. This pause allows the newly formed committee to gather their bearings as a unit, before acting as one. Once the committee has chosen their chairperson or leader, I move in. I approach the chair of the committee and begin to lay a foundation for the duration of the committee's term. This foundation needs to be built on trust, genuine trust, for us to function cohesively. Once we have a solid foundation in place, we can then begin to prepare a strategy to implement our views.

Once I establish a stable relationship with the player's committee, the membership is soon to follow. I always do my best to lead by example, showing the association that I am supportive of their needs and concerns. It may sound simple, sometimes as simple as reading the collective bargaining agreement itself, but putting any of these individual pieces into motion is a challenge, in and of itself.

Once the committee chair, committee, and players are feeling comfortable, I can begin to include the other side—the management—both strategically and carefully. A mix of trust and good judgment must occur on my part for this process to be a smooth one. Trust is vital, and it is always my intention to serve both sides the best I can.

I am compelled to offer information to those above me, as well. Most of that group was on the hiring side of my position, and because of the hierarchy in place, I must honor those relationships. In my eyes, it all comes down to the real key to success: balance.

Under normal circumstances, keeping an even keel is not problematic. I believe the success of our joint progress is partly due to the preparations on both sides. From time to time, there can be an issue that needs a bit more coaxing on my end, to one side or the other. Although no one likes to lose an argument, we all know that most disagreements require compromise on behalf of both parties. That is the way of the world here in Symphony-land, and we all know it.

The real problem comes into play when I am called upon to offer information that I feel is unethical, or against my inner moral fibers. At the moment of the inquest, I must decide if it is worth sacrificing my integrity to appease the seeker, knowing I need to remain faithful to my beliefs. I will never allow my standards to be compromised, not for the orchestra committee or the management.

By standing firm and saying "No," I can compel both sides to find another viable solution, to relieve the conflict at hand. If there is no solution, no middle ground, I remain committed to upholding my original rooted integrity. It is my task, if not my duty, to work through the process with both sides. Although my stance may place me in a vulnerable position, I remain steadfast and uphold my principles.

I would think, after having a high success rate in my current position, that I would have the full trust of management. I am not new at this job and am a seasoned veteran in my field. Along with the 14 years of professional experience I have under my belt as personnel manager at the symphony, I also have over 30 years of contracting experience. Throughout the industry, I am known as a "people person." I have earned the respect of my peers.

"I am above the weakness of seeking to establish a sequence of cause and effect, between the disaster and the atrocity." Edgar Allan Poe

A couple of years ago, I witnessed a contracted musician (Ben) place pressure on a substitute (Pasquale), in what I felt was a ploy to circumvent dealing with me directly.

As a personnel manager, I am in charge of overseeing substitutes and their interaction with the membership, as well as reporting back to the principal of each section. In most cases, there is nothing to share. In the unlikely case I have something to report, we must decide on a proper approach.

When a substitute becomes the focus of recurring issues, a natural remedy is to remove the substitute from the hiring list, or to drop them toward the bottom. Either way, a message is sent to the player, and before long they become obsolete.

Because I am a skilled and seasoned professional, I was able to see through the personal and professional dynamics of what was unfolding.

On June 7, 2017, my contemporaneous notes (in part) state that there was an issue with shields which I resolved on the spot.

That evening, I received an email from Ben that was copied to the entire Operations Department, in which he requested that there be one shield for both himself and his stand partner at all remaining S14 services.

I confirmed the request for Ben, but not for his stand partner, as he needed to make the request himself.

My notes continue the next day:

June 7, 2017: 9:20 a.m.

- The rehearsals are in the Victoria Theater today. The set-up is vastly different from the set-up in Prudential Hall as a result, I asked Ben if he still needed a shield for the rehearsals. He said no, that he had already informed the stagehands of the matter. Digesting that Ben broke protocol by going directly to the stagehands, I asked him to send me an email recanting his request from the June 6 email. I felt the need to cover my bases.

  At 9:40 a.m., 20 minutes before rehearsal was set to begin, Ben asked if he could speak with me. We stepped to the side of the stage to begin our talk. As the conversation became very personal, I felt it might be better to talk in a more private setting. I requested we step outside of the backstage area to continue talking, and he obliged.

Once in a more suitable location, Ben asked me why I had requested an email confirmation from him. I was asking for backup, in the event there was any fallout for not providing a shield for the rehearsals. I wanted written proof that he was okay working that way in the Victoria Theater. He asked why I would make such a request

I felt the need because Ben has always treated me with disrespect and I felt the need to protect myself. I always wondered what did to Ben, to warrant such disrespect but knew that I would never get a response.

Digging down as deep as I could, I made what I thought was a great offer to Ben. I suggested starting immediately, right now, we can turn the page on the past seven years of troubles. I continued, all we need to do is respect each other. Please say yes, and a new chapter begins today. His reply was short and to the point: "I don't trust you." The conversation ended there.

Later that day, I was approached by a member of the Orchestra Committee. They attempted to discipline me for not placing a shield out for Ben. I told the committee member that it was Ben who informed the stagehands he didn't need a shield in the Victoria Theater. I reminded the committee member of what the protocol was for requesting shields. Those requests come directly to the personnel manager. I added that Ben didn't even have the decency to ask me.

After the conversation with the committee member, I wanted Ben's and my exchange to be in writing, for my protection. So later that day, on June 9, 2017, 4:03 p.m. I made a note of all events to date.

My contemporaneous notes state:

Ben did not use a shield for the Thursday, June 8 performance at the Prudential Hall. In the efforts to make things better for the remaining performances, I offered to switch the position of stand five with stand six, to provide maximum relief. I have done my job in looking out for my players, even those who don't trust me.

On Saturday, June 10, 2017, the stand and shield issue boiled over. After the performance, Pasquale approached me onstage as I was packing up the percussion equipment. With tears in his eyes, he stated over and over, "I don't want to lose my position with the orchestra as a substitute, I love playing here." I reassured Pasquale that he had nothing to fear and I would make sure that this issue would never come up.

On our drive home from our performance in Red Bank, I drafted an email to Ben. It wasn't until after I completed my draft that I received an email from Pasquale. In his email, he expressed a real concern about his position as a substitute as well as how he felt he was being used by Ben. This information from Pasquale corroborated what I already knew, but it was nice to have confirmation of what I had witnessed all week.

Based on that conversation and our email exchange, I felt the need to protect Pasquale and issue Ben a written warning, so that he would not make this kind of request of substitutes in the future. In my statement, I informed him that his actions were unconscionable and would not be tolerated.

Ten days after issuing Ben his warning, on June 20, 2017, I received a letter from a private attorney who represented Ben. The letter was sent to the local union, as well as my superiors at the Symphony. Ben's lawyer reprimanded me for my treatment of their client and boasted accusations of harassment for "many years."

The letter, like most from the desk of attorneys, was strongly worded and alleged many claims against me, including "years" of inappropriate remarks, "intimidation," and "targeting," of their client. They claimed that this created a hostile working environment that, if continued, would result in Ben pursuing legal action.

In disbelief, I called my boss and asked how the symphony was planning on handling the situation. After all, I am an employee of the organization, so the responsibility now falls on their shoulders to work out a solution.

After getting off the phone with my supervisor, Mr. Tiranno, I began to dig through Ben's personnel file. I read letters I sent to Ben of deportment, letters to my boss showing his offensive nature, all with supporting documents. My contemporaneous notes would always include details such as the day, time, as well as other moment-defining details.

Although I brought every infraction to Tiranno as they happened, he never responded to my complaints. Tiranno dealt with my issues by repeating one of his two favorite mantras: "Just take the high road," or, no less ridiculous, given the issue, "Stop, and count to ten." Tiranno's stoic responses only underscored what I have believed for years: that he did everything possible to avoid any confrontation.

I felt the need to further illustrate Ben's attitude to Tiranno, so I submitted more supporting documents. The documents highlighted only two of many instances of grave deportment, of which there were a plethora of examples.

When I presented Tiranno with my notes, I was looking for guidance and remedy, instead, he did not hold any council to resolve the matter at all. I felt let down at the lack of discussion, as it caused me great distress in having to resolve the issue completely solo.

Looking at substantive matters, the letter from Ben's lawyer was baseless and without merit. I considered hiring a private attorney to rebuke the false claims, but first thought it would be best to work with my boss.

I asked Tiranno to have Ben supply his contemporaneous, notes backing up his claims of "harassment over the years." If Ben suffered from my hand, I would imagine he would keep meticulous records describing each instance. These records would prove the timeline, they would show when I was abusive, the circumstances, what I said. Ben should have all of these facts in his notes.

Sir Arthur Conan Doyle wrote: "Once you eliminate the impossible, whatever remains, no matter how improbable, must be the truth." I knew the truth many years ago, when problems with Ben first began, and I knew the truth now. I just didn't wish to believe it. Tiranno found it easier to sweep any Ben-related matters under the rug rather than help resolve our problems.

Norway opened my eyes and propelled me to the only logical conclusion. Be prepared to get out while you still possess your dignity, integrity, and morals. Due to the lack of proactiveness on the part of Tiranno, I began to think that this situation was not going to end well. If at some point I am going to leave this organization, I am going to do so on my terms.

In the fall of 2017, just one week before the opening of the season, I asked—rather, I begged—for a response to the accusations levied against me in Ben's June letter. Two months have passed since my revelation in Norway, and now three and a half months have passed with no movement on Tiranno's part. How was I to begin the season with this dark cloud hanging over my head? It was up to management to resolve the issue, so we could all start the 2017–2018 season on the right foot.

Finally, Tiranno scheduled a meeting. I would soon learn it would be our only meeting on the subject. When I walked into the meeting at the Symphony office, I noticed that there was only one empty seat at the table, and the placement of that seat was located in between my two superiors. Seating placement is a tactic often used to intimidate people. I read about that strategy years before, so when I saw the layout, I was ready.

As soon as I sat down, there was no hesitation on either of their parts. From the start, Tiranno hammered me with questions, me while my other superior, von Asst looked on. To say that I felt Tiranno treated me with utter contempt and disrespect is an understatement. When I would not respond to such treatment, von Asst then joined in. Jointly, they swiftly directed the conversation and moved their agenda along.

One of their many ridiculous statements uttered by them was: "We have observed that you looked tired last season." I thought, rather distractedly, to myself: neither Tiranno nor von Asst has children, neither one knows what it is like to tend to the needs of children on a regular basis. They have no experience in dropping their 13-year-old son off at 6 a.m. swim practice, or sitting through their seven-hour swim meets, and then putting in a long day's work.

I am not insulting those without children, but need to illustrate that the responsibilities to one's family add another layer to life, as well as any job. "Did anything impede my judgment or production in any way? Was something missing in my production, were we ever short a musician on stage?" I replied.

Stymied by my response, they moved on to the next topic. They then informed me that they felt I needed to attend Human Resource training, to help me as their employee. Ah, a great idea, I thought, maybe things are turning around? I fully and immediately agreed and thanked them for the opportunity. Human Resource training has been something that I have been requesting for years. I understand how training can only help me as a manager, person, leader, husband, and father. I was delighted at the possibility of progress.

After agreeing to any time and place for training, I asked a follow-up question. "How are you planning to deal with the letter from Ben's lawyer?" I continued, "Please assist me, guide me, after three and a half months of waiting I would like some resolution on this topic." They had no thoughts of resolution and only reinforced their agenda. "This meeting is about you, and we believe *you* need Human Resource training." Of course, I agreed to train. They had nothing further to share and ended the meeting.

I left the office at precisely 10:22 a.m., perplexed. Management had scheduled a 90-minute meeting, yet we finished in less than 22 minutes— utterly appalling.

They knew, with absolute certainty, there was going to be no offer of resolution. It was easier for Tiranno to protect Ben than attempt to help or, God forbid, resolve the issue. I left the meeting feeling two things: one,

Tiranno strung me along for three and a half months; and two, I may never return to this job.

Feeling the pending doom, I engaged a lawyer to deal with the fallout from Ben's lawyer's letter, as well as to seek advice on what I perceived as imminent termination.

Just one week before the start of the season, management requested all the work files I had in place. That was the first time in 14 years they had made such a request. Those included all personnel hired for the next eight months, payroll files, email communications—the works.

Tiranno knew my work ethic and also knew that by the beginning of August, I would have 95% of all the extra personnel in place for the entire season. He needed those records before proceeding to carry out his plans. I shared with my lawyer; it was clear to me that my firing would follow shortly after I handed over those files.

At first, I refused to send them to the office. I then realized those files didn't belong to me—they belonged to the organization. It struck me that if I were a lawyer and I left the firm; all my case files would need to stay in possession of the organization. I reluctantly hit send on the drafted email, sending all the requested information. I felt deep down, that once Tiranno had the needed files, my time would be up.

Sure enough, before I was able to put my Geiranger plans into motion, Tiranno terminated me. I had been a loyal employee for 14 years, serving the membership while providing professional services to all during my tenure. Yet, management felt it was easier to release me rather than to deal with the real issue. Unbelievably, I learned of my termination in an email from my lawyer, a full day after it took place. I didn't even receive a personal call from my superior, Tiranno.

To add insult to injury, I was made privy to the send-off email Tiranno sent to the orchestra regarding my release. Tiranno didn't have the decency of thanking me for my years of service. He didn't wish me well in my future endeavors. Instead, he sent a callous message simply stating that I was no longer working for the organization, without any context nor explanation provided.

Just one day after the termination email was sent, the Player's Association issued a statement to Mr. Tiranno, expressing their dismay. The email was one that both criticized the manner in which Tiranno handled my termination, as well as thanked me for my years of leadership and service to the organization.

In the weeks to come, Tiranno even toyed around with his version of a severance package. But the offer was accompanied by pages upon pages of restrictions on my behavior. Statements such as "Employee agrees that if he attends a performance of the Orchestra, that he will not go backstage or interact with any Orchestra employee, other than his spouse. The employee cannot greet any Orchestra employee by saying, 'Hello, how are you?' and respond to any similar inquiry, 'I am doing well,' or words to that effect."

I was shocked to read the statement that highlighted the reason for my termination: "The Orchestra will truthfully state that employee was terminated from employment because he was not performing up to the Orchestra's expectations."

Anyone who thinks for a moment that they can control me is sadly mistaken. Although Tiranno knows me, knows I am a man of high integrity, he had never considered that I would never accept an offer which would prevent me from upholding my right to freedom of speech. Just as I would always follow my moral compass on personnel issues, the decision not to accept the absurd severance package was unquestionable. I keep my freedom, and as a result, can share this story with you.

With my mind made up, visions of Geiranger came flooding back, her beauty and serenity offered me a feeling of tranquility, showering my mind and body with peaceful embraces.

As time passed, I deduced what was at the root of Tiranno's actions, as I had witnessed his behavior for nearly 20 years. Every time I would sign a freelance work contract, I felt his disdain for me grew. His jealousy manifested itself through his curiosity, as he would often press me on the details of my outside work. Over the years, I felt the less I would share, the deeper his wariness grew.

I was always looking for some project we could work on together, as I knew this might help our damaged relationship. Looking through my notes, I saw that there had been many times where I did pitch projects to Tiranno. My records reflect that he would always meet me with resistance. Perhaps he felt if the board learned that I had secured work for the organization, it would reflect poorly on him.

Along with his feelings of jealousy, I don't think he could ever accept my level of success, either on or off the stage. I cannot recall, ever, not even once in 20 years, an instance when he congratulated me on a particular soloist performance. During my 20-year tenure, I appeared as co-soloist in two Tan Dun Concerti (The Water Concerto and The Earth Concerto). In both instances, I took my position in front of the orchestra, side by side with the primary soloist. Tiranno never offered one word of congratulation or appreciation. I perform at the highest level attainable, focusing on my contribution as a performer, all the while concurrently managing the orchestra members and their needs.

A few days after the release of my first book, *Onward and Upward*, I came to work only to witness half of the orchestra reading it. I was thrilled by what I saw, a complete show of support from my peers. I recall feeling so emotional, I found it difficult to swallow for several minutes. Even board members were reading my book, and some of them asked me to sign their copy. With complete humility, I obliged.

Each year, the Symphony would host a silent fundraising auction. The head of the auction task force pitched this scenario: the winner of the $195 auction would receive a signed copy of *Onward and Upward*. Additionally, they would get to spend a complete rehearsal with me, both on stage and behind the scenes. There they would experience the full gamut of my abilities and the scope of both my jobs. Of course, I agreed. Every year we held the auction, there was always a winning bid.

Even in my show of support to the organization, the very act of accepting the auction details seemed to add yet another level in Tiranno's displeasure toward me. His apparent detestation for me was on the rise. Not to my surprise, Tiranno never congratulated, or even acknowledged, that I wrote a book, never mind what dedication it took to complete such a task.

Tiranno posits that my termination had to do with me "not performing up to the Orchestra's expectations." Anyone who has witnessed our interactions over the years knows, without question, this is a complete falsehood.

In the long run, I am the winner. I retain my life, my dignity, and my moral compass remains untouched. I am not sure how I didn't "live up to the orchestra's expectations," as no one ever addressed my abilities or lack thereof. In all my years of being an orchestra personnel manager, I experienced only two administrative reviews, both within the first few years of my tenure. These reviews carried more than 87% membership approval rating. Additionally, Tiranno never offered criticism that would have caused me any concern.

I hope Ben, Tiranno, and von Asst will have a chance to reflect on how their treatment of me reflects on them as both professionals and human beings. Karma is like a boomerang; it is not about punishment. Instead, it is about learning life's lessons. In the end, everyone must face the consequences of their actions. I wish the three of them continued success; if they keep with their current conduct, they will need whatever edge they can get.

Gratitude

I claim to be a simple individual liable to err like any other fellow
mortal. I own, however, that I have humility enough to confess
my errors and to retrace my steps. ~Mahatma Gandhi

On October 10, 2017, just a day after I posted on social media my thanks
and gratitude to all of my musicians for the years of collaboration, an
onslaught of support and love came flooding in, in response to the
announcement.

From my Facebook page (https://www.facebook.com/jim.neglia), dated
October 10, 2017

Thank you!

It has been my honor to serve the musicians of the NJSO
for the past 14 seasons. Now it is time to focus on my
contracting work around North America and beyond. Until
our paths cross again, I wish you continued success!
536 likes – 344 comments

My posting projects a great deal, in just a few words. It reflects one's necessary professionalism when leaving a position after many years of service.

I had to think, doesn't it reveal that anyone who would not offer their thanks to a decade-long coworker, demonstrate the dissatisfaction within themselves? Von Asst and Tiranno are nothing less than ingrates and deeply disturbed souls. If they treated me this way, it is a reflection of how they hold the rest of their staff, musicians and board members in the same low esteem; there is no other rationale possibility.

Why one leaves a company is not the real issue of importance. Rather, it is what they and their partners accomplished over the course of their tenure that matters. One would expect at a bare minimum offering of "We wish Jim good luck in all future endeavors." That should be part of any public, professional send-off. Anything short of that reveals how poorly managers regard their employees.

I have an extraordinary amount of compassion for those who didn't offer me their good wishes, upon my departure. They cannot, or do not, live up to the professional standard of any organization or leadership role, under any circumstance. I have complete and utter compassion for their unfortunate, convoluted ways, and lack of better judgment. I have learned that they are just not capable of those human traits. For that, I am filled with empathy. I hope that one day, they might see the light.

With that being said, hundreds of colleagues' expressions of gratitude came flooding through on my Facebook page. Their comments show their visceral reaction to my departure from the organization, as well as to me personally, who guided them for so long. The comments ranged from simple statements like *Onward and Upward Jim* to *In Boca al Lupo, I know you will be fabulous in all you do!*

Other remarks that really touched me were *keep inspiring people along the way, as you do! - Thank you for your professionalism, advocacy, and most importantly, your friendship. Working with you was always a wonderful experience - Thank you for all of your hard work and true dedication to your colleagues. Onward and Upward my friend!*

Some the really touched me were more personal in comment, phrases like *You are such a welcoming and hospitable person, and a real mensch ~ you are a straight-ahead guy, much appreciated in this crazy industry.*

> "Thousands of candles can be lighted from a single candle, and the life of the single candle will not be shortened. Happiness never decreases by being shared." ~Mahatma Gandhi

Inspiring comments that moved me to my inner core: *Always loved you and your kind spirit. You are an inspiration for us all.*

Touching comments which included: *~ I know if you're making this move, it's the right one for you. I will miss your hand on my shoulder as you survey the stage - finding solutions to problems before they even take form. Getting to know you has been one of the most treasured perks. I can't wait to marvel at your new adventures ~ The orchestra will never be the same, and you are the best personnel manager I've ever had the honor of working with. Your next adventures will be incredible, and I can't wait to hear about them all! ~ You are the consummate personnel manager, dealing quickly, honestly and fairly with such a wide range of issues, and always with collegiality and good humor. I can't imagine anything but very satisfying success for you in your new endeavors. ~ You will be greatly missed. Thank you for all the ways you took care of us. You always went over and beyond for everyone. ~ YOU welcomed me into the Orchestra, and YOU were the one that made it feel like a family. Your constant upbeat and positive presence is irreplaceable and is a monumental loss for everyone. You are the very best at what you do and inspiration to me! Your future colleagues are truly lucky people, and I envy them! ~ A great personnel manager is never surprised by a situation, but rather anticipates what might happen and provides solutions before a problem crops up. One of your finest attributes. ~ I am sure everyone will miss your great energy and work ethic. May the wind always be at your back! ~ You're an amazing manager with such a caring, energetic and positive attitude towards your musicians.*

Just a few of the hundreds of comments from my friends and colleagues. As each comment appeared, it only solidified my belief that it takes only a few words to show one's respect and appreciation towards another. I am genuinely grateful to everyone who took a moment to comment on my post, as all those who shared will be forever immortalized not just on my social media page, but also in my heart.

Moving On

"You can only lose what you cling to."
~Buddha

As people learned that I had more time on my hands, the phone began to ring, and my email inbox grew.

Within a few days, I began working on new projects, some of which require travel. I could now accept these offers without hesitation, as a full-time position at the symphony no longer encumbered my time. The decision we made in Norway was working out better than we had imagined. In fact, there was a sharp increase from the first month of my departure, to month three of my Renaissance.

Amazed, but not shocked as to what is transpiring, I embrace all changes or adjustments, knowing this is just the beginning. Happy to return to working for myself, where I first began years ago, I embraced the energy and direction.

Moving forward, I know I have one more decision to make. The question is, should I retire from performing? I am an "all in" kind of person no matter the topic or circumstance, my approach remains diligent on doing everything thoroughly, entirely, wholly, and with passion. With that being said, full retirement at my age concerned me. However, reducing or liquidating my percussion inventory became a real possibility.

The thought of actually selling my studio was daunting, but with my all-encompassing mentality, I took my trusty iPhone and methodically began taking pictures of every item in my studio. I took over 450 photos, capturing each instrument, stick, mallet, and beater.

After uploading the photos to my website, I started writing a short description for each item. This task alone took several days to accomplish, as I wanted to be thorough, without being too wordy. The next step introduced me to the real labor intensive of this process— gathering prices for all 450 plus items.

There are many factors to take into consideration when coming up with a retail price. I thought the instruments should be worth more than just the retail value because I had performed on them during my 30-plus year career. Once I woke up from that dream, and logic settled in, I hit the Internet to gather price information for each item.

However, most of the prices I found on Google were conflicting. What now? I and decided to take an average of the top four amounts listed and cross my fingers.

Pricing each item took a few more days of diligent detective work. The goal wasn't to make money by pricing items out of range but pricing my collection at a price that would attract a sale of all of the items. Although it was challenging to come up with the right prices, I did my best to be fair and impartial in the process.

With the entire project complete, the web link was ready for public consumption. All I needed to do was hit "upload to the Internet," and I would be up and running, ready for offers.

I felt the need to sleep on it for one more night, before making my absolute final decision, although I knew what I had been doing the past six days nearly round the clock was the correct move. I prepared an email, inviting all my friends, colleagues, students, enemies, whoever, to my website. With that prepared, I also developed a notice of instruction on my site, sharing how to make purchases. It read:

"Liquidating my studio of percussion instruments! All instruments were used professionally over the past 30 plus years. All instruments well maintained. I am not giving anything away, just downsizing. If you are interested, email me."

Additionally, I copied my website link to my Facebook page, offering more exposure. There weren't a million dollars of equipment, but there was enough there to purchase at least a BMW 7 series, and I didn't want to just give instruments away. We were talking about a considerable amount of investing over the years, and now was time for a return on my investment.

Although I was nervous about parting with my instruments, I was excited at the thought of downsizing at this stage of my life. I always imagined I would downsize when I was in my sixties, not fifties, but circumstances cannot be avoided or ignored. I rolled with my reality and pressed the magic button.

Within minutes, my email box was flooded, as was my Facebook messenger account. I also listed the instruments on a classical percussion Facebook page, as well as vintage drum page. Within 20 minutes, my computer lit up like a well-oiled pinball machine!

Within an hour of going live in cyber-world, a fantastic thing happened. Someone told me that they would like to come over and perhaps make an offer for the entire collection. What?! After swallowing hard, I replied that I was home and they were welcome to visit at will.

By then, I had sold a good deal of my collection to various orchestra and ballet companies throughout the United States and Canada and had put aside those items I elected to keep for myself.

About an hour later, Peter arrived, assessed what was remaining, and made me an offer. Although the number was a bit less than what I felt the collection was worth, I accepted it. I needed to consider that he was taking everything for resale and assuming all of the risk. I merely agreed to a buy-out.

Another consideration for making a deal with Peter, as opposed to selling on my own, would be the need to collect all funds from the purchasers and ship the items. Knowing that selling on my own included finding boxes, tape, packing items, making trips to the post office, filling out insurance forms, and many other tedious tasks, I was happy to make a deal with Peter. Plus, when you have an inventory of over 450 instruments, you need to set aside time to actually find the item you are selling. That requires labeling of all instruments, keeping track of your list, and then taking each piece off the website once that item sells. Needless to say, I was *really* happy to make a deal with Peter!

What is the remedy? Sell the bulk of collection to one person, cash and carry. On November 15, 2017, Peter arrived with a U-Haul truck, as well as three workers to remove the inventory from my basement. In return, I received a stack of cash. The long-awaited return on my investment had arrived.

Epilogue

"The measure of a life is a measure of love and respect
So hard to earn, so easily burned
In the fullness of time
A garden to nurture and protect" ~Peart

Much like downsizing, my thoughts all started to solidify with firm resolve. My thoughts were clear, in focus, and perhaps for the first time in a long time, brutally honest. I was no longer worried or frightened about slowing down, changing modes, or rediscovering my life goals.

After experiencing my near-death ordeal, my health became the primary focus of my thinking. I knew it is time for me to move on and save myself from a life that controlled me, to a life that I control. Regarding my work, I wanted a more peaceful life. It was time to see what other opportunities were waiting for me and focus more on those already established relationships.

Reflecting on the past 18 months of opportunities, I compiled a list of accomplishments which I felt I could continue to grow. On my list are The Game of Thrones Tour, Zelda, Symphony of the Goddesses, Final Fantasy, and Hans Zimmer Tours. Along with those tours, I had worked with various organizations on the *Nike* experience, Michelin Tires festivities, as well as the New York Fashion show with Michael Kors. All of these productions fell well outside of the non-profit model and become part of my new focus.

I feel my needs have come full circle. Much like Francesco Paolo experiencing contentment through his love of family and music, our needs revert to the essentials: a place to live, food on our table, and love in our hearts and home.

Not only are we sure we don't need so much, my wife and I both realize that we don't want so much. I am sure the transformation we lived through while in Norway helped guide us with many of our decisions. Without question, the fjords made a direct and significant impact on Sasha and I.

We decided to sell many things from our home, items that have not been in use for months, if not years. We even decided to sell our large house and move into a luxury condominium. Downsizing took place, all with happiness and liberation. We were feeling free from the shackles which held us in place for the past two-plus decades and found real comfort in purging more than half of our belongings.

Adding to our new existence, I was no longer in a hurry to find a cover player with an hour's notice. There were no more pending grievances to respond to, no one calling in sick, no more stifling work condition. I no longer needed to deal with incompetent bosses, nasty CEO'S, insecure librarians, sometimes defiant, arrogant co-workers. Instead, there was an astounding serenity which was beginning to umbrella our lives.

Upon this realization, I started, almost immediately to experience inner peace and calm, the same feeling I had experienced while sitting on the shores of Geiranger. It is a feeling that is hard to put into words, a feeling that may come but once in a lifetime. If it happens, you don't want to blink. I didn't miss the opportunity. I made sure to seize it.

I was living just as I did when I first started my career over 30 years ago, working for myself with no one to answer to. My goodness, I feel great.

I feel rejuvenated, refreshed, free, and happier than I have been for years. Spared the jail cell from which I lived, shown the light which leads me from the darkness of negativity to the shores of Norway. What a blessing, how profoundly fortunate! I am feeling gifted, watched over, cared for, fortuitous, and enlightened.

A very long time ago, I made a promise to myself which went something like this: "If you wake up in the morning and dislike what you have to do that day, then perhaps it is time to do something else." I did just that. I took my own advice and followed my heart on a path leading Onward and Upward!

About the Author

Jim Neglia is a veteran force in the Performing Arts. He has been a working percussionist as well as music contractor, personnel manager and music coordinator for more than 30 years, working closely with some of the best-known names in the industry.

During his career, he performed with the New Jersey Symphony, New York City Opera, and performed live on the radio program All Things Considered. Jim's career also took him abroad working in 27 countries as a solo and orchestral percussionist. He has appeared and performed in motion pictures, "I love NY", with Christopher Plummer as well as "Joe Goulds Secret" with Stanley Tucci.

Jim keeps a busy schedule as an International Music Coordinator for multiple organizations and tours.

He resides in Florham Park, New Jersey with his wife Alexandra, and two sons Phillip and Daniel. For relaxation, he enjoys reading, writing, collection autographs of classical composers.

Made in the USA
San Bernardino, CA
03 June 2019